THE HOUR OF THE GODDESS

Chitrita Banerji grew up in Calcutta, received her master's degree from Harvard University, and now lives in Cambridge, Massachusetts. She spent many years as a journalist, editor and translator. Her other books include *Bengali Cooking: Seasons and Festivals* and *Life and Food in Bengal*.

Her articles, columns and short fiction have appeared in *Granta*, *Gourmet*, *Gastronomica*, *Boston Globe*, *American Prospect*, *Calyx*, *Petits Propos Culinaires*, *Phoenix*, and *Boston Magazine*, and she has received awards for her papers at the Oxford Symposium of Food and Cookery.

THE HOUR OF THE GODDESS

Memories of Women, Food and Ritual in Bengal

CHITRITA BANERJI

PENGUIN BOOKS

PENGUIN BOOKS

USA | Canada | UK | Ireland | Australia
New Zealand | India | South Africa | China

Penguin Books is part of the Penguin Random House group of
companies whose addresses can be found at global.penguinrandomhouse.com

Published by Penguin Random House India Pvt. Ltd
7th Floor, Infinity Tower C, DLF Cyber City,
Gurgaon 122 002, Haryana, India

Penguin
Random House
India

First published by Seagull Books Private Limited 2001
First published in paperback by Penguin Books India in
association with Seagull Books 2006

ISBN 9780144001422

Typeset in Perpetua by Mantra Virtual Services, New Delhi

Printed at Repro Knowledgecast Limited, India

www.penguin.co.in

For all the generations of Bengali women who created, enhanced, and preserved a culinary tradition of excellence and innovation

CONTENTS

In New England, as I look out of my window, there is more colour in the leaves than on people during the autumn. The farm stalls and supermarkets proliferate with vegetables and the prospect of warm kitchens is once again welcome. Autumn, in this northern latitude, is the time to start wrapping up, to draw inward from the far-flung activities of the summer, start the school year, and buckle down to the serious business of living.

Thousands of miles from my window, there is a place where autumn is the antithesis of such earnestness. In eastern India it is the holiday season, marked by three major religious festivals. In that lush tropical delta crisscrossed by countless rivers—my native region of Bengal—there is nothing misty or wistful about autumn. It comes riding vigorously on the heels of a receding monsoon. It dissipates the cloud cover, banishes the enervating moisture from soil and air, and lets the earth bask under a kindly sun in a blue, cloud-flecked sky. Its primary icon is that of the many-armed goddess Durga, a resplendent figure, all gold and red, riding a lion and carrying ten different weapons in her ten hands, a potent symbol of victory and hope who destroys the dark demon Mahishasura.

The ebullience of nature and the liberating effect of the holiday season is complemented by another potent pleasure. Autumn, and later winter, is the time to eat well, especially to indulge in the richer foods that are so hard to digest in the heat of the summer or the persistent dampness of the monsoon. The presence of the goddesses elevates food to an almost suprasensory experience. Many Bengali favourites, including meat, are also cooked for them. Once the food is ritually offered and supposedly accepted by the deity, its very nature is transformed. However illusory it sounds, I know that a major part of the pleasure of many festive foods is associated with the ritual of offering. As if, by preparing and offering food, the earthbound worshipper can bridge the gulf between mortality and divinity.

Whenever I think of the autumn festival of Durga, and of the subsequent ones honouring the goddesses Lakshmi and Kali, I am overcome by the aroma of hot, puffy *luchis* (deep-fried puffed bread), of *alur dam* (slow-cooked spicy potatoes) nestling in a glistening, dark, tamarind sauce, of golden *chholar dal* (yellow split peas) spiced with cumin, coriander, cinnamon, and cardamom, its thick texture flecked with tiny coconut chips fried in sizzling mustard oil. The richness of meat cooked in a fragrant, spicy sauce extends pleasure to the edge of sin. My tongue wraps itself around the cool memory of a rice pudding made with milk evaporated to a rich, pinky-brown creaminess and combined with fragrant *gobindabhog* rice, crushed cardamom seeds, and pistachio morsels.

As with eating, celebration too is marked not by restraint, but by boundless enthusiasm. The autumn festivities are about inclusion and community participation. The bursting bounty of the fields is matched by the joyful throngs, dressed in vibrant new clothes, milling about the streets and visiting the neighbourhood pandals, temporary enclosures where images of the goddess are enshrined for the festival. Celebration in Bengal is inevitably chaotic, exuberant, cacophonic, and above all, public.

My memory of these festivals is always connected to that of my first Christmas in America. Arriving as a student in the autumn, I had kept my homesickness at bay by imagining that Christmas would be a compensatory event. I anticipated the same kind of energy, laughter, and fragrance that festivals had always meant for me. Instead, I found myself inhabiting a ghost town. All the students in my dormitory, except for two other hapless foreigners like me, had gone home. The cafeteria had shut down. Even the city streets were deserted. Christmas, I discovered, like other festivals here, was a very private family event behind closed doors. The joys of giving, receiving, merrymaking, and eating were off-limits to all but the inner circle. Walking the deserted streets, I went past houses whose windows glowed with many lights. I saw people gathered around tables, the flickering flames of candles. I laughed to myself, wondering what would happen if I rang the doorbell of a house and asked to come in.

Of course I did no such thing. But the pent-up nostalgia for a lost autumn returned forcefully in the desolate winter. I was suddenly filled with a determination to hold on, to capture memory in every shape and form so that neither time nor distance made a void in my heart. No longer afraid of feeling sad, I concentrated instead on remembering every autumn ritual that had sent me forward, year to year. The aromas of signature festive foods came and wrapped me in a comforting cocoon. But I realized with a pang that I did not know how to cook any of them. They had always appeared magically from the loving hands of my mother and relatives. I decided then to learn without any waste of time. Eagerly, I wrote to my mother, asking for recipes and directions and embarked on an experimental period of long-distance cooking lessons.

It has been many years since then. The very different beauty of the New England autumn has, over time, become as precious to me as the remembered season of Bengal. And now, when my calendar shows the beginning of another festive period—three days of worshipping Durga, to be followed by Lakshmi and Kali—and I remember how incense smoke and the crushed petals of marigold, hibiscus, and tuberose lend their scents to the redolence of cooked offerings and delectable family meals,

I, too, am connected. Messages from the goddesses come rustling through the rich-toned foliage of sugar maple, oak, and beech; and memory swells potent, as the aromas, textures and tastes transport me back into a different world.

LUCHIS

FOR SIX PEOPLE

INGREDIENTS

500 gm (1 lb) of flour
2½ teaspoons of ghee or peanut oil
300 ml (10 fl oz) of water
1 teaspoon of salt

METHOD

I usually take 500 gm (1 lb) of flour, which makes five or six luchis for each person. For big eaters you need more. I put the flour on a large tray or platter, preferably with raised sides, add salt and ghee or peanut oil and mix them well. (You can make sure that the oil is sufficient by taking a handful of the flour and pressing it tightly in your fist. If the flour adheres in a lump, the oil is right; if it falls apart, mix in just a little more oil.) After the oil has been well mixed in, the flour has to be kneaded into a dough with water. I generally start with 300 ml (10 fl oz) of water, which I keep adding slowly to the flour as I gather it in from all sides of the tray to make one lump. If you find you still need a little more water, then carefully sprinkle some over the dough. Too much will ruin the dough, making it too thin. Once the flour has become a neat lump, the hard work of kneading starts. The more you do this, the better the quality of dough and the puffier the luchi. Usually ten to twelve minutes of forceful kneading with both palms, pressing down with the base of the palm, is good enough. At the end, the dough should feel elastic when pulled apart. It is then divided into the little round portions called *nechis*. Each one is smoothed over between the palms and pressed to flatten it, then rolled out on the board as thin as possible to make a 12.5 cm (5 in) luchi. The traditional way is to dip the nechi into a bowl of oil and then roll it out so that it does not stick to the rolling board. However, the oily surface can be slippery, and the easier way out is to dust each nechi very lightly with flour before rolling. A perfect circle is hard to achieve, but this is the ideal. As I roll the luchis out, I keep them side by side on a large dry platter or sheet of newspaper spread on the kitchen counter. It is best not to let them overlap too much because they might start sticking to each other. Once seven or eight have been rolled out, I put the karai on the stove, heat 120 ml (4 fl oz) of peanut oil in it and start frying. To do this well, hold one side of a luchi, lower it gently into the oil—still holding it—and set it afloat like a paper boat. This way you avoid a splash and prevent the thin disk of flour from crumpling up. As it puffs up like a balloon, turn it over with a spatula, fry for a minute more and gently lift it up along the side to drain off all excess oil. A good luchi should not be too brown, but creamy-beige in colour. I keep rolling the rest of the nechis in between bouts of frying. Hot luchis should never be covered, or they will go limp.

CHHOLAR DAL

FOR FOUR PEOPLE

INGREDIENTS

250 gm (½ lb) of yellow split peas
3 bay leaves

3 whole red chillies
One half of a whole coconut
2 tablespoons of sizzling mustard oil
1 ½ teaspoons of whole cumin seeds
½ teaspoon of ginger paste
½ teaspoon of ground chilli
1 teaspoon each of fresh ground cumin and coriander
400 ml (13 fl oz) of water
3 teaspoons of sugar
1 tablespoon of ghee
2 teaspoons of ground garom mashla
Salt to taste

METHOD

For chholar dal to feed four people, my mother would weigh out the yellow split peas and cook them in the pressure cooker with double the amount of water, bay leaves and whole red chillies. She left the cooker for about fifteen to twenty minutes on a high flame. By then the cooked dal would be of a thickish consistency and the individual grains would be soft but unbroken. This she would empty out in a bowl and set aside. Then she would take one half of a whole coconut and pry out half the flesh from the shell. The brown skin at the back would be painstakingly peeled with a sharp knife. If you find this too hard, you can try soaking the coconut for ten minutes in a bowl of hot water. Once peeled, the coconut would be chopped into tiny pieces and fried in the sizzling mustard oil in a large karai until they turned pink. She would add whole cumin seeds to the coconut and fry them for a couple of minutes before adding ginger paste, ground chilli, fresh ground cumin and coriander and salt to taste. Once all this had been fried for two to three minutes, she would pour the dal into the karai. (On bad days when there were no freshly ground spices and she had to fall back on powdered spices, she would pour in the dal after frying the coconut and the whole cumin, adding the other spices later.) The dal would be checked for salt, water added, and the whole mixture assiduously stirred until the grains were mashed. Some sugar would be added; this is a dal in which the sweetness should be a little pronounced. Just before removing the dal from the fire, she would add ghee and ground garom mashla.

ALUR DAM

FOR FOUR TO FIVE PEOPLE

INGREDIENTS

500 gm (1 lb) potatoes
3-4 dry red chillies
3-4 teaspoons of whole cumin seeds
3-4 teaspoons each of cumin and chilli powder
1 ½ teaspoons of tamarind extract
3 tablespoons of mustard oil
2-3 bay leaves
1 teaspoon of panch phoron
A tiny pinch of asafoetida
¼ teaspoon of turmeric powder
400 ml (13 fl oz) of water
Salt to taste

METHOD

To make alur dam, boil and peel the potatoes—in that order—and quarter them. Take dry red chillies and whole cumin seeds. Toast them in a dry frying pan over a medium flame until the chillies are dark brown. Remove and grind them as fine as you can in a pestle or on a grinding stone. (If, however, this seems too much trouble, take 3-4 teaspoons each of cumin and chilli powder and roast them together in a frying pan. The taste and flavour will be pretty good, though not as good as that of freshly ground spices.) Next, take tamarind extract and mix it smoothly in a bowl with 60 ml (2 fl oz) of hot water. Set aside. Heat mustard oil in a karai and throw in bay leaves, panch phoron and a tiny pinch of asafoetida crumbled between your fingers. As the panch phoron stops sputtering, put in the potatoes and sprinkle the turmeric powder over them. Stir repeatedly until they turn golden brown and pour in the water. Once it comes to the boil, reduce the heat to medium and simmer for four to five minutes. Then add salt to taste, 2 teaspoons of the roasted spices and the tamarind paste. Stir thoroughly for another three to four minutes and taste to find your balance of salt and sour. You can add more or less of the roasted powder depending on your tolerance for hot food. If the gravy becomes too thick, or too sour, more water can be added.

2

FEEDING THE GODS

Feet. My face almost upon them. A wide assortment of bare adult feet, rough and calloused, well-tended and manicured, plump, delicate, flat and arched. Feet shuffling, tapping, or dancing in rhythm to an ecstatic chant. I see them as I scramble on bare knees on a cool, silky-smooth floor, my left hand holding up the front of my skirt to form a pouch, my right arm darting in and out between the feet. I am six years old, maybe seven, and I am hunting and gathering *batashas*.

Each successful lunge and capture fills the small hollow of my palm with the fragile, round, meringue-like batashas—airy, brittle puffs of spun sugar, brown or white in colour, depending on the kind of sugar used. Hunting for batashas was the obligatory ritual which ended the evenings of *kirtan*-singing that punctuated the narrative of daily life for my intensely religious family in Calcutta. As Bengali Hindus of the Vaishnava sect, my grandparents worshipped Vishnu the Preserver as chief among the gods. In scripture and myth he appears as the destroyer of evil, liberator of the oppressed, master of incarnations, lord of many names: Krishna, Keshab, Madhav, Narayan, Hari. But, I was taught, he is also a lover, and often willing to put aside his power and glory for the sake of closeness with his mortal devotees. Singing kirtans—medieval lyrics about Krishna and his earthly love, Radha the milkmaid—was one way for us to achieve oneness with him.

The lyrics sung, the group of singers (mostly male) would begin a protracted choral chant of two words, 'Hari Bol', 'take the name of Hari,' in an escalating crescendo of notes. In their fervour, some even stood up and swayed to the rhythm, eyes closed, arms raised. Some fell into a trance. That was the signal for my grandmother to come in with an enormous brass platter filled with batashas and perform the playful ritual I so loved— Harir loot. Handfuls of batashas were thrown up in the air and came spinning down to the floor. Immediately, the listeners (family, neighbours, and friends) would fall to their knees, each person becoming a pillager intent on gathering as much of the sanctified loot as possible. It wasn't until I was much older that I appreciated the serendipity that allowed the same word, loot, to mean the same thing in two languages.

For several years, I was the only child in our large rambling house in south Calcutta, where my parents lived with the extended family of grandparents, uncles, and aunts. As the daughter of a working mother, I was often in the care of my grandmother. In spite of her many chores and responsibilities, she always found time for two things—worshipping the gods morning and evening, and telling me stories. The stories were spun out of an enormous alternative universe she seemed to carry in her head, a world of gods, demons, heroes, witches, kings, princes and, of course, beautiful princesses. But to the telling of the tale she brought such unquestioning faith that I had no problem travelling with her between the mundane and the extraordinary.

There we were, on a summer morning, sitting on the floor of the atrium-like central space on the second floor from which all the rooms opened out. My grandmother's left foot pressed down on the flat wooden base out of which rose the arc-like blade of the Bengali *bonti*, on which generations of women have cut their vegetables. A large basket of vegetables lay on one side. I sat on the other, watchful, eager, ready with questions. It was the same in the *thakurghar*, or prayer room, set aside for the gods. Morning and evening the gods received their dues in this room—a variety of seasonal fruits, store-bought or homemade sweets, batashas, raisins, and leaves of the *tulsi*, or holy basil. And if I was around, any part of the daily rites of offering my grandmother performed could spin off into stories, fantastic or real.

Food and worship have been interconnected in Hindu thinking from ancient times. In one of the *Upanishads*, the human soul, freed from mortality, is described as roaming the universe, chanting joyously, 'I am food, I am an eater of food.' Durga, goddess of deliverance, is eulogized in hymns as she who exists as nourishment in all creatures. In the early creation myths, the first offspring of Brahma the Creator is Agni (fire), who emerges from his mouth and is therefore an 'eater of food'. And it is in order to meet Agni's ravenous hunger that Brahma rubs his palms to produce the very first offerings of milk and butter. That was the origin of the Vedic practice of pouring oblations into the fire in order to ensure the birth of one's own progeny. And when this high-fat diet becomes too much even for Agni's fiery digestive system, he gives himself our equivalent of colonic irrigation or a high-fibre diet, by consuming an entire forest, for instance, as described in the *Mahabharata*!

Through the medium of offering food to the gods, the earthbound worshipper finds a metaphor for offering the self that is dependent on the same sustenance. In our house, the humans could only eat their first morsel of the day after the gods had been fed. Although the images are of many different gods and goddesses, star status went to two human manifestations of Vishnu—Gopal, the chubby, smiling infant, often depicted as stealing cream and curds from the kitchen of his foster mother Jashoda, and Krishna, the handsome, flute-playing youth, entwined with his beloved Radha. The bronze statue of Gopal sat directly on the altar. But Krishna and Radha—he carved out of a densely black stone, she from golden-white marble— had a more mobile existence. Every night the lovers were put to bed together in an exquisitely carved wooden bed, complete with bedposts and snow-white mosquito net. In the morning, my grandmother would ceremoniously raise the mosquito net, lift the images out of bed, and install them on the throne reserved for them on the altar.

Like so many rituals, the offering of food to the gods was always preceded by meticulous aesthetic preparation. I would sit quietly in a corner and observe my grandmother as worshipper. First, she pulled out a round stone slab, sprinkled water on it and rubbed it with a small bar of sandalwood. Instantly, the room was filled with the ineffable aroma of devotion. To this was added a smoky fragrance as incense sticks were lit. Flowers she picked every morning were dipped in the sandalwood paste, touched gently to her forehead, and laid out at the feet of each image, to the silent iteration of ritual and personal prayers. Finally, the batashas, fruits, and sweets were set out ceremoniously on several plates and offered collectively to the gods. Petrified in man-made images, the latter could never refute our assumptions about them. And so a seamless sequence bound us firmly through the pleasure of partaking—offerings were made, the gods supposedly accepted them, and the sanctified food, *proshad*, was then consumed by the worshipper to bridge the gap between mortality and divinity.

One of the things I learned by experience was that no food for the gods could be touched or tasted beforehand, however strong the temptation. Human desire and saliva destroyed the purity of the offering. Why, I asked one morning, after my wrist had been slapped for trying to sneak a section of orange. What was wrong with finding out how something tasted before offering it to the gods? That's what we did for our guests, didn't we? And, I said, warming to my theme, if Krishna loved us so well, wouldn't he be moved that we wanted to share something we knew beyond doubt to be delectable?

My grandmother turned her head slowly and looked at me. A lifetime of family squabbles and many betrayals had stamped her angular face with a guarded passivity, not bitterness. But her large, expressive eyes always lit up when she talked to me about Krishna's love, so real for her. In her usual fashion, she avoided a direct answer, but started on one of her numerous stories about Krishna's childhood in pastoral Brindaban.

The last surviving child of a dispossessed king, Krishna had been left in the care of a milkman and his wife, to be hidden from a murderous uncle. The little *avatar*-prince grew up with the children of other farmers and cowherds, in a world totally removed from the trappings of royalty. Often, in the course of grazing their flocks, the boys would happen upon a particularly delicious mango or some other fruit. Instead of gobbling down the whole thing, they would always turn to Krishna, their natural leader, and offer him the half-eaten fruit with all the depth of their love.

The unspoken inference was that some liberties were permissible for the bucolic youths in a mythical past, but not for the rest of us. Something in me could not accept this without verification. On a blistering summer afternoon when everyone at home was taking a nap, I stole into the thakurghar. Cupped in my hands were several plump, juicy lichees, my absolute favourite among fruits. Carefully, I knelt in front of the altar, peeled the biggest lichee, its juice squirting out joyfully as the translucent white flesh was released from the rough, bumpy, pink skin. Leaning forward, I took one sweet, fragrant bite of pulp and juice before holding out the rest of the fruit to Krishna as he dallied with his Radha on the throne. My chest constricted with fear and curiosity. For a second, I closed my eyes. Would I be struck dead for this flagrant transgression? Or would he accept me as a playmate, like the ones he had grown up with?

Finding that I was still alive despite my impudence, I opened my eyes and looked at the image of Krishna. Was there a responsive flicker in the beautiful elongated eyes carved in that gleaming black face? I no longer remember. But I do have this memory of bringing my hand back to my face and slowly, deliberately, finishing the rest of the fruit with an extraordinarily intense satisfaction. There were no doubts in my mind about the divine sanction of that fruity morsel. Could there be a truer experience of love?

Offerings, whether of food, or the more metaphysical aspects of the self, were not merely the means of keeping the gods happy or buying salvation for ourselves. In my mind, they are strongly associated with a sense of unrestricted joyfulness, and a heightening of gustatory pleasure. Familiar food somehow became extra delicious when I tasted it as proshad. Perhaps that derived from my awareness of my grandmother's intense pleasure in presenting offerings to Krishna, whom she perceived more as a friend than a distant god. Sometimes, when the two of us sat together after evening worship, she would expound her notion of religiosity as I listened openmouthed: God is being, consciousness, and bliss. Worshipping Krishna is knowing him, rejoicing in the love you feel for him. And since you cannot be in this mortal world without food, you must feed yourself and Krishna, with love and with joy. Remember, you are food, because the god who made you is also food. And in order to live, you must love him every day with food. Give him what you love most and you will find it tastes so much better afterwards. Now then, what will you feed Krishna tonight?

She smiled at me. It was a game between us as we sat

undisturbed. Everyone else was busy talking, cooking, listening to the radio, singing, or reading. Soon my mother would call me to have supper and go to bed. But there was this little window of time to be enjoyed with the gods. For my grandmother, at the end of a busy day's work, this was the space to be enjoyed exclusively, territorially, as her own. None of her adult children or daughters-in-law claimed her place in this room, although there were plenty of tussles over control and authority in the kitchen, the hiring of servants, the allocation of joint resources, the planning of social or religious festivities. In this one room, she was still absolute mistress and unquestioning worshipper. And I was the one person she welcomed wholeheartedly.

So, what would it be, for Krishna and for myself? I sat and stared at the array of peeled and cut fruits and the expensive sweets from fancy stores laid out before the altar. But when it came to the crucial choice of what I loved best, I always found myself reaching for the small marble plate containing the humble daily offering of batashas. How could you prefer anything else to the one thing that could be eaten endlessly?

On special occasions, such as Krishna's birthday, there were more elaborate offerings. Huge vegetarian meals were cooked at lunchtime and offered to Krishna before being served to family and guests. One of the most delightful offerings of this day was made from the extracted pulp and juice of the ripe *taal*, the large, strikingly fragrant fruit of the palm tree. The intensely sweet, saffron pulp is mixed with ground coconut and rice flour and made into crispy, sweet fritters—a supposed favourite of Krishna's adoptive father in Brindaban, Nanda. All of us, adults and myself, knew the song about Nanda dancing joyfully as he ate these delicious fritters. An alternative preparation was a chilled pudding made by boiling milk down to a semi-solid consistency and mixing it with the saffron pulp and finely ground coconut.

As I grew older, many factors contributed to a diminishing sense of joy and festivity in our family life. My grandfather's death put an end to those glorious evenings of kirtan-singing; the singers had mostly been his friends. Occasionally, one or two of my aunts would spend an evening singing the beautiful, familiar lyrics. The family would gather and listen. But these were sessions of muted devotion, of remembered loss—all sense of occasion, of a robust, almost rollicking joy in expressing faith and communion, were absent. Gradually, a slow attrition took over. Several of my uncles moved into their own homes. Comparatively isolated in her widowhood, my grandmother did not have the heart to organize festivities as she had in earlier times. Krishna's birthday came and went—always in the middle of the rainy season—but there were no twenty-four-hour marathons of kirtan-singing to celebrate the event. No bustling activity in the kitchen to prepare for guests those elaborate vegetarian lunches: hot, smoking *khichuri* (rice and *dal* cooked together with fragrant spices like bay leaf, cinnamon, and cardamom); sliced eggplants fried crisp; fritters made of seasoned mashed potatoes shaped into little balls, dipped in a batter of chickpea flour, and fried in oil; a vegetable medley flavoured with whole five-spice mix and dry red chillies; pressed squares of *chhana* (curdled milk solids) floating in a glorious sauce of ground ginger, cumin, coriander, cloves, cardamom, and cinnamon.

After my parents moved to their own home, I found myself even more distanced from the celebratory, worshipful life of my childhood. The academic pressures of a super-competitive high school and an expanding universe of books, ideas, and friendships, took me farther and farther from the mythical world of Krishna, Radha, cowherds, gods, demons, and miraculous happenings. My mother set aside a small room in our house to worship the gods and continued the same rituals as my grandmother, but for me, they became simply a part of the daily routine, like bathing or eating, instead of intersections with another reality.

All the friends I made in the elite college I went to came from families very different from mine. A few far more wealthy, and most far less observant of the rituals of devotion. Some of the boys took great pride in showing off their 'liberation' from traditional custom by ordering beef (absolutely forbidden to Hindus) in the cramped Muslim restaurants we frequented in search of their famous kebabs. The contemporary intellectual enthusiasms, derived very much from the West, were also antithetical to faith, ritual, and myth. At a time when young people in America were questioning the 'establishment' and gearing up for anti-war protests, students in Calcutta were damning their own system and looking for iconoclastic answers in varying leftist persuasions. Although I myself never acquired strong political affiliations, I entered and remained in a terrain of scepticism utterly alien to the self-forgetful joys of loving Krishna and making him offerings.

SIMPLE KHICHURI

FOR FIVE PEOPLE

INGREDIENTS

500 gm (1 lb) of atap rice
500 gm (1 lb) of roasted moong dal
60 ml (2 fl oz) of mustard or any other cooking oil
2 teaspoons of ghee

4 sticks of cinnamon, 2.5 cm (1 in) long, 4-5 whole cardamoms
and 4-5 whole cloves for garom mashla
2 bay leaves
A liberal pinch of whole cumin seeds
A piece of ginger 4 cm (½ in) long, chopped fine
2 whole green chillies
1½ teaspoons of turmeric powder
Salt and sugar to taste

METHOD

The rice and dal, rinsed separately under running water in
a colander, are left to dry on a flat surface for about fifteen
minutes. This process makes them easier to cook and,
anyway, in Bengal, we never cook anything without rinsing
it first in water. While they dry I put on the kettle so that I
have ready the hot, though not boiling, water I need to add
to the khichuri. I heat the oil in a medium-sized, heavy-
bottomed deep cooking pot, add the garom mashla and bay
leaves and wait for a couple of minutes, without stirring
them, for the fragrance to be released by the heat before I
throw in the cumin seeds and chopped ginger. These I stir-
fry for a couple of minutes, then add the half-dried rice and
fry it for two to three minutes. Finally I add the roasted
moong dal and the turmeric and stir the mixture for another
two to three minutes before pouring in the hot water. The
level of water should generally be 4 cm (1½ in) over the
rice and dal. If necessary, more hot water can be added
towards the end, depending on how thin you like your
khichuri or if the rice and dal are sticking to the pot. But a
lot of water at the beginning will make a mishmash of the
grains. Once the water comes to a boil, I add salt and sugar,
reduce the heat to low and cover the pot. Generally it takes

about twelve to fifteen minutes for the khichuri to be ready. To avoid sticking and even the slightest burning, which ruins the flavour, I keep checking from time to time and stir the mixture thoroughly with a spatula. If needed, I add a little more hot water. After ten minutes of cooking, it is a good idea to test the grains of rice and dal. When they feel nearly ready, I throw in the green chillies, check for salt and sugar, wait till the consistency is just right, add ghee and remove the pot from the stove. The earlier you add the chillies, the hotter the khichuri will be, for the stirring will blend them in.

BHUNI KHICHURI

FOR THREE TO FOUR PEOPLE

INGREDIENTS

500 gm (1 lb) of rice
250 gm (½ lb) of roasted moong dal
4 medium onions, finely chopped
2 teaspoons of ground ginger
2 tablespoons of chopped ginger
Garom mashla as for the simple khichuri, but crushed lightly
3 bay leaves
1 teaspoon of freshly ground cumin
1 teaspoon of whole cumin
7-8 ground chillies
120 gm (4 oz) of raisins
175 ml (6 fl oz) of ghee
Salt and sugar to taste

METHOD

Rinse and dry the rice and dal as for simple khichuri. Then heat the ghee in a pot and throw in the whole cumin with 2 bay leaves. As soon as they turn brown, add the crushed garom mashla and, a minute later, the chopped onions and ginger. Stir-fry till brown and add the rice . Lower the heat to medium and keep stirring until the rice makes popping noises. Then add the dal, fry for some more time and pour in the hot water, enough to cover the contents and stay almost 2.5 cm (1 in) above. Again, one has to be careful with the water, particularly because this khichuri has to be dry and fluffy, not soggy and mushy. A little more water can always be added if needed. As soon as the water comes to a boil, add salt and sugar and the green chillies, then lower the heat and cook, covered, for about five to six minutes. Check the salt and sugar balance at this point, adding more if needed, before adding the ground ginger and ground cumin as well as the raisins. Then add the remaining bay leaf, cover the pot tightly and reduce the flame to the barest minimum. If the khichuri looks too dry, this is the time to sprinkle more hot water over it. From time to time over the next four to five minutes, shake—never stir—the covered pot carefully, so that the grains will not stick to the bottom. When done, the bhuni khichuri will be very fluffy and should give off a complex aroma, heavier than that of the simple khichuri.

Many people love to add extra dollops of ghee to their platefuls of simple khichuri, although in these days of cholesterol fears, lemon juice squeezed over the top is also used to add zest. The bhuni khichuri, however, has too much ghee and spices to need any extra seasoning.

PAANCHMESHALI

INGREDIENTS

250 gm of potato

250 gm of brinjal

100 gm of patol

100 gm of green beans

½ cup of shelled green peas

¼ cup of oil (preferably mustard oil)

1 teaspoon of panch phoron

2 teaspoons of ground ginger

Salt to taste

1 teaspoon of turmeric powder

2 or 3 green chillies, slit lengthwise

METHOD

Cut all the vegetables into small cubes (or lengths for the beans) and wash them, but keep them in separate piles.

Heat the oil in a karai. Throw in the panch phoron. As soon as the seeds sputter and release their flavour, add the ground ginger and stir well. Now add the potatoes, beans, patols and peas, and stir vigorously for five minutes. Add some salt and throw in the brinjals. Stir vigorously for a couple of minutes and add the green chillies. Reduce heat to low and cover tightly. No water should be added to this dish. The vegetables will release their moisture and that should help the harder items like potatoes and beans to cook while the flavours intermingle. Uncover karai and check from time to time to see how the vegetables are progressing, stirring thoroughly each time. If the softer vegetables are done and the potatoes are still hard, sprinkle some water and keep tightly covered for five minutes. Uncover again, check for salt adjusting if

needed, and remove. The texture should be dry.
Serve with rice, luchi, or chapati.

3
PATOLER MA

Childhood is full of mysteries, even the most mundane aspects of daily living piquant with the promise of revelation. The daily ritual in our house that intrigued me most was the processing of spices on the grinding stone. We did not have a refrigerator then. It was considered an unnecessary luxury—something only the very rich would waste money on. The buying, processing, and cooking of food, therefore, was a major part of the daily household activity. And the preparation of spices for cooking—the transformation of seeds, herbs, and roots into smooth pastes, each with its unique colour—was, to me, the most magical part of the daily rituals of food.

My parents and I lived on the third floor of my grandparents' large, rambling, three-storied house in south Calcutta. It was a typical Bengali extended family, the house humming with the comings and goings of parents, uncles, aunts, and frequent visitors. The kitchen and pantry happened to be on the second floor, directly below our rooms on the third. And every morning I listened for the sound of the up-ended *shil*, a large, flat block of stone with a deeply pitted surface, being lowered to the concrete floor from its rest against the wall. That was the signal that our daily maid, called, in the customary manner, Patoler Ma (or mother of Patol, after her offspring), had arrived and was starting on her chores. Once she had ground the spices, the cook could start on his job of preparing daily meals for our large family.

I think it was the juxtaposition of Patoler Ma's skeletally thin body—especially her stick-like arms and legs—with the massiveness of the grinding stone, that gave me my very first sense of the unfairness of life, and particularly the unfairness that women contend with every day in many traditional societies. She seemed so pitifully inadequate to this Herculean task of grasping and moving the stone into the appropriate position for spice grinding, while our male cook looked on, never offering to help, despite his obvious advantage of size and strength. She hardly ever missed a day's work and the routine never varied—spice grinding was the first chore of the day. The stone and Patoler Ma pitted themselves against each other every morning, year after year, and she inevitably won, for otherwise I would not have seen the magical transmutation that was wrought on that subjugated stone.

An unspoken method seemed to guide her as she set about this daily ritual—as if she was an artist preparing her palette for the day. Whenever I could, I went downstairs to watch her getting ready for her task, squatting in the small passageway in front of the kitchen. First she sprinkled lots of water on the oblong stone surface of the shil and vigorously wiped it off with the side of her palm. The water fell in large drops along the edges of the stone, forming a translucent pattern on the floor. Then she took the heavy, pestle-shaped, rough-hewn bar of stone, the *nora*, and wiped it down the same way. Now she was ready for action.

The cook had already set out the spices on a large, white enamelled platter with a raised cobalt-blue rim. Patoler Ma liked to start with the rock-hard lumps of dried turmeric. That was the base ingredient around which you built the colour and texture of your food. And it was the hardest to process. Bang, bang, bang she went, pounding away at the recalcitrant lumps with the nora held vertically in her right hand, while the left hand balanced the pieces. I watched and trembled at the possible mischance of the stone landing on her thumb or finger. But miraculously, that never happened. Sometimes, a piece rolled off the stone and fell to the floor. But sooner or later, they were all beaten down into smaller granules, their tint deepening into sunflower yellow as they mixed with the water on the surface of the stones. Sprinkling more water on the turmeric, Patoler Ma then switched motions. Holding the nora horizontally in both hands, she proceeded to grind the spice into a sun-bright paste, while the signature odour of turmeric filled the air. As I watched her—body leaning forward between legs folded in the squatting position, a look of intense concentration on her lean face under a huge topknot of black hair, arms vigorously moving back and forth with the nora—I thought of her as a woman warrior, despite her frailty.

The transformation of dried red chillies was another fascinating process for me. There was always something threatening about them, whether I saw them sitting in a bowl or being picked out from the large jar on the kitchen shelf. Unlike the fresh green chillies that were often used whole in cooking and were also served as an accompaniment during meals for those who wanted to add more zest to their food, these dried chillies seemed to be infused with a sinister potential. Perhaps it was because of the intensely pungent odour they produced when the cook fried them in oil as a flavouring for certain dishes. You could be up on the third floor, but they still inflamed your nasal membranes and plunged you into an epidemic of sneezing. I had also been burnt by their fire once when neither the cook nor Patoler Ma was watching. Picking up a chilli I broke it open with a little snap. Seeing the small, pale seeds spilling out, I took some and put them in my mouth. It brought tears to my eyes; and the trauma was intensified when I rubbed my eyes with fingers on which minute particles of chilli still adhered.

And yet, Patoler Ma seemed to have no fear of these lean and fearsomely pungent missiles. Breaking off the stems, she firmly placed them on the stone, sprinkled water over them, brought the nora down and started moving it back and forth. I watched as the skins split open and yielded up the seeds, which, in turn, became pulverized and blended with the now moistly red, rejuvenated flesh of the chillies. Soon, she was scooping out the smooth red paste from the stone and placing it on the waiting plate—next to the rounded ball of yellow turmeric. Often, I surreptitiously looked at her hand. The fingers were stained with the colours of the spices, the predominant tinge being yellow. And I marvelled at the nonchalance with which she went through the day, never afraid of touching her eyes or lips or nose with fingers on which the burning essence of chillies might linger. Perhaps such accidents did happen, but life was tough for Patoler Ma and she had to get on with it, despite a runny nose, teary eyes, or stinging lips.

By the time she finished, the rounded balls of paste on the white plate added up to a whole spectrum of hues. The dull, mousy browns of ground cumin and coriander were often enlivened by the creamy whiteness of Indian poppy seeds (so different from the black poppy seeds used in the west). But the most intriguing colour was that of ground mustard. This dark, Indian variety has an exhilarating sharpness when it is freshly ground. To dispel its bitterness, mustard seeds are ground together with one or two fresh green chillies and a touch of salt. Sitting near Patoler Ma, I often leaned closer just to catch the mouthwatering whiff of this titillating combination. The final product, a yellowish brown tinged with green, looked, and often was, good enough to taste on its own. On hot summer afternoons, my mother sometimes took sour green mangoes and peeled, seeded, and sliced them. The slices were then mixed with salt, mustard oil, and the ground mustard left over from the morning's cooking. The result was an epicure's delight, to be savoured by itself, one delicate piece after another, the tongue shivering with both shock and joy, but always craving more.

On the infrequent occasions when we ate meat, usually for Sunday afternoon lunch, Patoler Ma had to contend with ingredients that had their own moisture—onions, garlic, and ginger—as well as the most aromatic elements in our kitchen—cinnamon, cardamom, and clove. The noise of stone on stone was very different when the element between them was a juicy allium or a fleshy root like ginger. Their fluid-filled substance cushioned the shock and was reduced to paste with relatively little effort. But of course such ease came at a price. By the time she finished with them, Patoler Ma had tears streaming down her face and had to sniff vigorously to control her runny nose. So it must have been a relief to switch to the harder, sharper, smaller and intensely fragrant spices that we called garom mashla. As she hammered away at the combined pile of cinnamon, cardamom, and clove, before making them into paste, I would draw deep breaths to hold in as much as possible of the scent that was released.

Once I asked Patoler Ma if these were not her favourite spices when she cooked for her own family, since they smelled so good. She turned towards me with the saddest smile I had ever seen. 'People like me can't afford to buy garom mashla,' she said, 'we only handle and smell it in the homes of people like you.' The starkness of the statement at first puzzled me, then brought home to me the iniquities of poverty and our day-to-day acceptance of it. What must it feel like, I wondered, to spend so much energy in processing ingredients that you may desire but could never obtain? My child's brain came nowhere near an answer, but the question lived with me and edged me towards the curiosity about other lives and other worlds that consumes all writers.

The days of the shil and the nora are long gone from my life—as far away, today, as my lost childhood. Now, as I pour

out powdered spices from capped bottles or plastic bags, I mourn
the absence of freshness and intensity that only fresh, stone-
ground spices can produce, and miss the earthy magic of
transformation wrought by stone and human hand. In my
modern American kitchen I use different electrical gadgets to
change whole seed or root into paste and powder, but it is a
mechanical process. In this kitchen, there is no white enamel
plate with an array of spices waiting to be transformed into the
palette of life by someone like Patoler Ma. But despite the lack
of immediate and visible alchemy in the preparation of my daily
food, I do not yearn for that long-gone ritual of spice grinding.
For whenever the image of that colourful plate of spices rises
before my eyes, it is inevitably overlaid by a film of another
colour—that of Patoler Ma's sadness.

4

A DOSE OF BITTERS

My grandmother was a great believer in traditional herbal lore, according to which, a regular dose of bitter vegetables would protect you from all the physical ills with which nature assaults the feeble human body. She insisted that one of them be always served as a starter at lunchtime. The bitter leaves of an ancient Indian tree, neem, was the springtime favourite. In our family, a favourite delicacy was *neembegun*. Its simplicity is stunning. The neem leaves, delicate, coppery, feathery as they emerge in spring, are fried crisp in a little oil and set aside. Eggplant cubes are then sautéd with a little salt, and when done, are mingled with the leaves whose papery crispness infuses the plush vegetables. Eaten with rice, neembegun is an addictive starter, the bitterness underscored by a secret sweetness. As an added bonus, bitter vegetables are also supposed to calm rage.

At first, I would protest bitterly against the bitter stuff—I was only a girl, I had no rage to speak of, why did I have to go through this torture? But that never cut any ice with my grandmother. Girls, she said, were doubly vulnerable, because they were inclined to suppress their anger. All that unspilled rage was absorbed by their livers. And the only way a girl could keep her liver healthy was by eating right. I figured out early on that it never paid to go against her dictums, however weird they sounded. Like her children, I too came to accept the daily dose of bitters with stoicism. Neem was the easiest to get, for we never had to buy the leaves from the market. A huge tree flourished in a corner of the garden. Every spring it was a sight to cheer up the most irate of mortals, covered with small, glossy, coppery, serrated leaves, handfuls of which would be plucked just before cooking.

Over time, though I never reconciled myself to the other bitter vegetables I was forced to eat, I did acquire a fondness for the neem concoction. Sitting down to lunch, I would pull forward a portion of the delicate, long-grained, jasmine-white rice on my plate and mix it with the neem and eggplant, relishing the contrary textures of crispy, crumbling leaves and soft, plush eggplant as I worked my fingers through all of them. The combined taste became the subtlest of addictions—bitter, salty, sticky, succulent, all at once. And then, as if to compensate, would appear the daily delectations—fish, meat, vegetables, and legumes, shining with dark mustard oil, golden with ghee, kaleidoscopic in colour, subtly spiced, fragrantly flavoured.

'The Bengali seems to have always had a sweet tooth,' says K. T. Achaya in his seminal work, *Indian Food*. And indeed, a traveller in other regions of India is certain to hear many comments about Bengali sweets, the complexity and variety of which testify to a people's addiction. Literature and historical narratives are also replete with references to the sweet-loving Bengali. Of course, it is not difficult to understand this addiction. Give a crying baby something sweet and it will usually calm down. The human tongue seems to have a primal affinity for sweetness. Milk, the primary nourishment, has a pure and sweet undertaste.

The exact opposite may be concluded about bitterness. The taste buds cringe, the tongue recoils, the brain revolts into rejection. The human baby lulled by sweetness, instinctively and strongly rejects anything that tastes bitter—a reaction that has led to folk practices like putting quinine on the nipple to wean a nursing infant or on the thumb of an older child to help it grow out of excessive thumb-sucking. Language and metaphor reinforce this. Unpleasant facts, experiences, and relationships are 'bitter' in many languages across different cultures.

How then to account for the eagerness and delight with which we consume some of the most bitter of nature's gifts? An acquired taste, say many. But that merely skims the surface of the mystery. Why bother to go to the distasteful trouble of acquiring such a taste when other, more delightful, eating experiences abound? And in the best tradition of mystery novels, the plot thickens when one examines the culinary practices of sweet-loving Bengal, where bitter vegetables are eaten as gustatory treats, and not as a symbol of penance or to commemorate past sorrows, as in the case of the bitter herbs served at the Passover seder to symbolize the bitter times the Jews endured in Egypt.

In considering the paradox of the sweet-addicted Bengali's equal addiction to bitterness, I am reminded of miele amaro, a bitter honey that Sardinia is famous for. It is made from the flowers of a humble bush called corbezzolo. In early winter its branches are covered with small dark red fruits resembling strawberries, which has led to the erroneous English name, strawberry tree. Miele amaro is produced in very small quantities and is as expensive as it is cherished. To me it is the perfect representation of the intersection of tastes, which lends mystery and delight to food.

The traditional midday meal in Bengal is incomplete without a starter like *shukto*, which is a vegetable medley with the primary accent on *karola*—a knobbly, green-skinned, white-fleshed vegetable of the cucurbitae family, often inaccurately called bitter gourd. Despite the addition of spices like ginger or mustard or ground poppy seeds, the shukto is unmistakably bitter. Why would a hospitable people like the Bengalis invite a guest and assault the palate? Cynics believe it is an instance of the Bengali's peculiar, devious thinking. Start off a meal with something bitter and anything you present afterwards will taste ambrosial. But the obvious relish with which Bengalis mop up their portions of shukto with rice belies this theory. For the true test of a cook in Bengal lies in how good a shukto she or he can make.

Of course shukto is not the only way to use karolas. The versatility of Bengali cooks is demonstrated in many other preparations. Very young karolas can be steamed, mashed with a little salt and a spoonful of pungent mustard oil, and eaten with plain rice. For the fainthearted, the bitterness of unadulterated karola can be mitigated by mixing it with mashed potatoes. Roundly sliced and crisply fried slices of karola can be a lighter starter than shukto. Chopped into slim, inch-long pieces, the karola can be combined with eggplant, daikon radish, and potatoes and made into a stir-fry, flavoured with panchphoron (a whole spice mixture of mustard seeds, black cumin, cumin, fenugreek, and fennel seeds) and spiced with green chillies and ground mustard. On a hot summer day, a pot of yellow moong dal can be given a refreshing twist with the addition of chopped karola, green chillies, and ginger.

Like all children, I too recoiled from my first encounters with shukto. My mother, however, was firm about what I had to eat. Neither tears nor defiance got me anywhere. And despite my grandmother's theories about karola being good for the liver, I simply saw the portion of shukto on my plate as one more example of adults exercising unfair power over the child. But years later, as a chronicler of Bengal's food history, I found evidence about our belief in the healthful properties of bitter vegetables that went back more than a thousand years. An eleventh-century collection of proverbs and sayings, attributed to a wise woman named Khana, recommends eating karola during the Bengali month of Chaitra (mid-March to mid-April), when the unforgiving heat of the tropical sun is at its worst.

Khana was an amazing figure. The daughter of a renowned mathematician named Barahamihir, she defied tradition that limited education to men and became as proficient as any of her father's male students. Her particular genius lay in interpreting natural data as they related to cropping practices, soil fertility, and harvest projections. Over time, her recommendations constituted a manual for Bengali farmers.

Bengali narrative poems of the fifteenth and sixteenth century also harp on the medicinal qualities of bitter vegetables. There I found the word shukto to derive from *shukuta*, the dried leaves of the bitter jute plant. Herbalists and shamans believed it to be a powerful antidote for excessive mucus in the gut, as manifested in a common tropical affliction—dysentery. The theory has been forgotten. But the practice has become part of cuisine. The leaves of the jute plant—once Bengal's most important cash crop, from which, in the days before synthetic fibres, burlap sacking was made for international shipping—are now eaten fresh, though they are not as common as karola and their somewhat slippery texture, reminiscent of okra in a gumbo, is not to everyone's taste.

In today's globalized world, neem is the ultimate symbol of the war between profiteering multinationals and indigenous peoples living by their local natural resources. The European Patent Office recently revoked a patent held by W. R. Grace (one of the offenders in the Woburn, Massachusetts case of dumping toxic chemicals) for manufacturing fungicide from the products of the neem tree. Indian farmers proved in court that their age-old practices already included such uses. But in the traditional Bengali kitchen, far from the turmoil of international lawsuits, neem leaves have long been a valued food item.

Neem leaves, moreover, have a virtue beyond taste, beyond aiding the liver, even beyond serving as a cure for many skin ailments. Take our gardener, whose face was riddled with pockmarks. He was the rare survivor of a smallpox epidemic in his village that had killed everyone in his family except him and a widowed aunt. The only thing that had kept him from going mad during the burning, itchy torture of the disease, he told me, was the soothing sensation of neem leaves brushing against his face and body. His aunt spent hours brushing his whole body with tender twigs of neem leaves tied together like a little broom. And from time to time, she would sponge him down with water in which neem leaves had been boiled, or sprinkle it on him.

And in the twilight zone between life and death, neem has the power to cleanse the living of the touch of the dead. I happened to learn about neem's power in this area through a death in the family. Things were not too sophisticated in those days. No vans or hearses to carry the dead. You just laid the body on the bed, rounded up as many men as you could, and walked all the way to the crematorium where the corpse would be burnt to cinders and the bed given away to the untouchable doms who did the grisly work of building the wood pyre, breaking the corpses' recalcitrant joints, and gathering the ashes for eventual disposal in the river. On the way to the crematorium and back, the whole group would chant the name of the lord in its funerary evocation, 'Bolo Hari, Hari Bol!'—a surefire way to get past sluggish crowds and knotty traffic, and, for nervous believers, to avoid the evil attentions of supernatural hoverers.

We stood on the second-floor balcony late that evening, my mother, grandmother, and I, waiting for the funeral party to return. The growing sound of chanting announced their impending arrival. My grandmother rushed downstairs, calling to the cook to bring the things she had kept ready. Ever curious,

I followed. Each mourner was given water to wash his hands and feet. He then touched a spill of burning newspaper, and chewed a raw neem leaf my grandmother held out. Only then did she stand aside and let him enter the house. Why, I asked her a few days later, but never got a satisfactory answer. In some distant lore, somewhere dimly in the collective memory, neem must have acquired a greater than therapeutic status, cleansing mourners of the touch of the dead. Creepy as I found that wash-touch-chew ritual at the doorway, I had no problems distancing myself from it in a few days. Before long, I was once again enjoying fried neem leaves and eggplant with rice at lunchtime.

SHUKTO

FOR FOUR PEOPLE

INGREDIENTS

500 gm (1 lb) of cubed or sliced mixed vegetables such as potatoes, brinjals, sweet potatoes, green papayas, local radishes, flat beans, green bananas, patols, ridged gourds or jhinge and bitter gourds

2 + 1 tablespoons of oil

½ + ½ teaspoon of panch phoron

1 tablespoon ground posto or poppy seeds

3 tablespoons of mustard (ground fine with a touch of salt)

1 tablespoon of ground ginger

2 bay leaves

2 teaspoons of flour

2 teaspoons of ghee

3 teaspoons of sugar

Salt to taste

METHOD

We often feel you cannot have too much of shukto. For

four people we usually take about 500 gm (1 lb) of cubed or sliced mixed vegetables. The thing to remember is that the bitter gourds should be sliced very fine and should not be more than one fifth of the total quantity of vegetables. Once all the vegetables have been washed, heat a little oil in a karai and sauté the bitter gourd slices for three to four minutes. Remove and keep apart. Add a little more oil to the pot (the total amount should be about 2 tablespoons) and throw in ½ teaspoon of panch phoron. A couple of minutes later, add the rest of the raw vegetables, stir for four to five minutes and add enough water to cook the vegetables. Keep covered until they are cooked, add the fried bitter gourds together with salt to taste and the sugar. Cook over high heat for another three to four minutes and remove from the stove.

To spice this dish we use ground posto, mustard and ground ginger. This is added in the second stage of the cooking, when 1 tablespoon of oil is heated in another pot, and another ½ teaspoon of panch phoron, together with the bay leaves and half the ground ginger thrown into it. Once this has been fried for a minute or so, the cooked vegetables with the gravy are poured in and brought to the boil. The posto and mustard are combined in a bowl with flour and a little water and the paste is added to the pot. After cooking these for three to four minutes, the ghee and the rest of the ginger are added. The salt and the sugar are checked, the whole thing stirred thoroughly to blend the flavours and the pot removed from the fire. The sweetness should balance the bitterness, so more sugar might be needed. It is up to the cook to decide how much sugar he or she wants to add; being Ghotis, we like our shukto to be sweetish, but others prefer it more bitter. The sauce should be thick, not watery, and whitish in colour. I find that the delicacy of flavour is heightened if the shukto is served warm rather than piping hot.

5

FOOD AND DIFFERENCE

The defining experience of my life has been close encounters with communities that were different from mine but had existed in close contiguity for centuries. The daughter of a family deeply rooted in the Indian province of West Bengal, I happened to form many close friendships in school with girls whose families originally came from East Bengal, the province that became East Pakistan after the partition and independence of the Indian subcontinent, and twenty-five years later, broke away from Pakistan to become Bangladesh. Stereotypes and biases reared their heads at every turn and, even when allayed by humour, never lost their sting. Food, cooking styles, and eating habits of rival communities were the most common topics for insults, jocular or vicious. Despite this, for me, in the course of life's journey, encountering and appreciating differing food habits and practices has led to unexpected enrichment.

East and West Bengalis have semi-derisive terms for each other—Ghotis for West Bengalis, Bangals for East Bengalis—used equally as proud badges of identification and loaded terms of pejoration. People take refuge behind these terms to justify all kinds of closemindedness. My family was so Ghoti, that when marriages were arranged, one important question was whether the prospective bride or groom was also an unadulterated Ghoti. When one of my uncles went off and married a Bangal, it created far more commotion than when another married an American.

The Ghoti/Bangal divide was my first experience of the power of bias. With one exception, all the friends I made during my school years in Calcutta were from Bangal families. As a result, I was at the receiving end of much goodnatured teasing about Ghotis, especially our eating habits. Food was much on our minds as we started the morning ride on the school bus. Since there was no organized school lunch unlike in many countries in the West, we would carry something small—a sandwich, some fruit, something sweet—for lunch. But the day's main meal of rice, lentils, vegetables, fish or meat, which is traditionally eaten in Bengal at lunchtime, was forcefed to us early in the morning to sustain us through the school day.

There we were, a gaggle of girls on a school bus, chattering, whispering and giggling. What we had just eaten was fresh in our minds. Many of us found getting ready in the morning a tiresome chore, often climbing into the bus with hair half-braided, belt untied, shoes unlaced—tasks to be finished during the ride. And so we often resented the time taken up by having to eat everything our mothers insisted was necessary for good nutrition. Rice, of course, was the staple. But in the houses of my Bangal friends, there could be no meal without the obligatory fish stew or *maachher jhol*, no matter how early the departure.

For those who don't know much about Bengali food, this fish stew has traditionally been the centrepiece of the day's main meal. But in a Ghoti household like ours, eating a meal without fish was quite common if time was short, or if the cook was late with the morning shopping. There were always enough things to accompany my rice—dal, vegetables cooked in many ways, even a quick omelette to provide the protein. So doing without fish on some days was no great deprivation. But when I said this, my Bangal friends roared with laughter. To them it was unthinkable to start the day without the sacrosanct maachher jhol. One might as well not eat. With condescension and sarcasm, they would proffer portions of their midday snacks to me, the poor deprived Ghoti. As I spent more time at their homes, I began to realize how pivotal the maachher jhol was to the Bangals. When I mentioned this to my parents and relatives, they would laugh and shake their heads at the vagaries of the rustics from across the border. When I asked for an explanation, I sometimes got answers that made sense (they come from the eastern part of Bengal where there are many more rivers and fish is plentiful, so they think of fish as a staple) but more often sarcastic jibes about an unsophisticated lot that came from the hinterland, had the uncontrolled appetite of peasants, and needed potfuls of maachher jhol to mop up mountains of rice. A frequently quoted doggerel referred to Bangals as subhuman.

My Bangal friends never missed the chance to laugh at the Ghoti habit of eating wheatflour *chapattis* at dinner which, I believe, came about because of the rice shortages in the sixties. The Bangals were proud of pointing out that despite the cost, they still ate rice for both lunch and dinner. It was only the Ghotis, who were not true Bengalis, that could switch to eating chapattis like those Hindi-speaking louts from the neighbouring state of Bihar.

Cooking styles were as varied between the two communities as food choice and priorities. The Ghoti trademark was the discernible sweet undertaste in the complex vegetable preparations that Bengal is famed for. To most Bangals, however, it was anathema. Ghotis, they said, were sissies, sweetening dishes that were meant to be hot, spicy, salty. If you want a sweet taste, why not eat dessert? In return, the Ghotis would sneer at the Bangals' predilection for chillies and rich, oily sauces that deadened the palate and left no room for subtle tastes. What do they know about food, I remember one of my great aunts saying, they put karola in their fish stew and make pudding out of white gourds!

Although I resented it bitterly when my Bangal peers ganged up on me and made fun of what Ghotis ate and how we cooked, by the time I was finishing high school, I had reluctantly come to one conclusion that I knew would infuriate most Ghotis, particularly if they heard it from one of their own. There is a greater degree of adventurous inventiveness in the cooking of

East Bengal. Perhaps it is because of the terrain, which is untamed, crisscrossed with the great rivers of the Bengal delta, rivers that rage with flood waters, erratically change course, blithely destroy human settlements, and throw up intensely fertile silt deposits that produce rich harvests for new settlers. Perhaps, under such a prevailing sense of uncertainty, you learn to make do with very little and yet turn it into something palatable to accompany the 'mountains of rice' needed for the voracious Bangal appetite. I say this knowing how dangerous it is, for it neatly echoes the stereotypes promoted by the Bangals themselves, of Ghotis being rigid, uninventive, and trapped in tradition!

Appreciation of Bangal cookery was reinforced during my late teens when my mother and I happened to embark on a parallel discovery (she was a skilled cook who delighted in learning new dishes from her East Bengal colleagues) of how the culinary imagination, rooted in a more rural landscape, can create succulent dishes out of humble ingredients. To take one example. Most of us, in cooking a cauliflower, would use the florets and discard everything else. Not the Bangals. As one friend demonstrated, the leaves can be chopped fine and turned into a delicious stir-fry flavoured with whole spice and dried red chillies. Potato and white gourd peel could also be treated the same way and tasted ambrosial as a starter with rice. In traditional Ghoti homes like ours, a fish called chitol was only half enjoyed. It is an extraordinarily bony fish, and so only the rich, oily, front portion of the fish, where the bones are large and easier to pick out, was considered edible. It was only much later that my mother learnt from one of her Bangal friends the trick of scraping the flesh away from the fine bones of the back portion, combining it with spices and mashed potatoes, and frying it in little balls, the glorious Bangal dish of *muittha*. It was a discovery that silenced the anti-Bangal commentary in our household for quite a while.

Perhaps the most extraordinary instance of the transmutation of the humble into the extraordinary was something I learned from the visiting grandmother of a friend of mine. I happened to drop by their home during the festival of Durga puja. On the fourth day of the puja, Durga (goddess of deliverance) is given an elaborate send-off with many offerings, usually expensive sweets and rare fruits. I was amazed to hear this elderly visitor reminiscing about her youth in a remote East Bengal village where the married women would prepare a humble vegetarian dish—stems of the water lily in a hot and sour tamarind sauce—and offer it to the goddess, beseeching protection from the disastrous fate of widowhood. Women in Bengal are famously fond of sour and tart preparations. Somehow, I felt, it was a supreme act of imagination and courage, to identify with the womanly aspect of this most powerful goddess, pushing aside the veil of divinity, and finding common ground in the appreciation of an inexpensive, unpretentious dish that would rarely be served to the males of the household, those mortal gods with immediate power to punish and reward. It created a new appreciation in my mind for those 'wild and untamed' inhabitants of East Bengal.

MACHHER JHOL

FOR FOUR PEOPLE

INGREDIENTS

500 gm (1 lb) of fish

4 medium potatoes

1 medium brinjal

10-12 kalai dal boris

1 teaspoon of turmeric powder

2 teaspoons of ground ginger
1 teaspoon each of ground chilli, cumin and coriander
1 teaspoon of panch phoron
5-6 green chillies
2 tablespoons of chopped coriander leaves
3 tablespoons of heated oil
900 ml (1½ pints) of water
Salt to taste

METHOD

In Bengal the favourites are the rui, the katla, or the mirgel, though any big fish can be made into a jhol. Once the head and the tail together with the last 10-12 cm (4-5 in) of the body are removed and set aside, the cook decides which portion of the body will be used for the jhol. The body of the fish is cut lengthwise, the front or stomach portion being called the *peti* and the back being called the *daga*. The peti is preferred for almost any dish since it is oilier and tastier. But the bony daga is ideal for the medium of the jhol. Whatever the portion chosen, it is then cut horizontally into pieces 2-2.5 cm (¾-1 in) in thickness. Since most families are unable to buy a whole fish, it is common in Bengali markets for the fishmonger to portion his fish and cut it to the specifications of the client. The fish is rinsed carefully to get rid of all traces of blood and slime, dusted with salt and turmeric and slowly fried in hot oil, two or three pieces at a time. The oil should be heated well before the fish is put in. The salt and turmeric are used, not only to reduce the fishy odour, but also because they prevent the fish from crumbling or disintegrating (this makes them almost inevitable ingredients for frying fish, prawn or crabs). Since the skin is left on the fish and tends to sputter in the oil, it is wise to keep your pan covered. Once the fish pieces have been lightly browned, they are lifted out and set aside to drain off all excess oil. If the frying oil has turned too dark, it has to be discarded.

Since two of the several vegetables we commonly use in jhols—patols and green bananas—may not be available everywhere, I'll stick to the certainties of potatoes and brinjals.

Take the potatoes, peel and cut them into long, flat, 1.25 cm (½ in) thick slices. The brinjal should also be cut into matching slices. If *boris* made of dried dal paste are available, 10-12 kalai dal boris, white in colour like the dal they are made with, are a must for this jhol. The boris have to be fried first in 3 tablespoons of heated oil. When they turn brown, lift them out by drawing them up along the sides of the karai so that all the oil drains back. The potato slices should also be lightly browned in the same oil and set aside. Then fry the panch phoron, add the ground spices, and stir for a couple of minutes. Add the brinjals and potatoes and pour the water into the karai. When it comes to the boil, add the pieces of fried fish, the boris, the green chillies and a little salt. The salt has to be added carefully because there is already salt in the fried fish. As the jhol keeps cooking, you can taste and adjust the salt. The whole thing should be kept on the stove until the fish and potatoes are tender—about five to six minutes. Finally, the coriander leaves should be stirred in and the jhol removed from the heat. The gravy should be thin and fragrant, but how thin or how spicy it is depends a lot on personal preference.

CHITOL KOPTA

FOR FOUR PEOPLE

INGREDIENTS

500 gm (1 lb) of fish
2 medium potatoes
½ teaspoon of ground ginger
1 medium onion, finely chopped
1 beaten egg
120 ml (4 fl oz) oil
Salt to taste

METHOD

For chitol kopta, the flesh is scooped away from the skin of the bony back portion with a spoon, but you have to be careful to move the spoon the way the bones are laid. If it moves against them, the bones will come away with the fish. To make the fishballs, first boil potatoes and mash them finely. Mix these thoroughly with the lump of fish. Though chitol, being very sticky, does not need this as a binder, I find the potatoes make the texture soft and fluffy. To the fish and potato mixture add some salt, ginger, and finely chopped onion and egg. Mix all of these together to make a tight dough-like lump. It should not be thin or watery. Divide it into 20 round or oval balls, patting each smooth between the palms. Then heat oil in a karai, and deep-fry the fishballs in it. In the hot oil they will swell up like little balloons, though they shrink later when taken out. These koptas can be served by themselves as an appetizer or snack, or just as an item with rice and dal. But mostly they are put into a thick gravy before serving with rice. For this, you need:

2 medium onions, finely chopped
½ teaspoon of ground ginger
1 teaspoon of chilli powder
½ teaspoon of turmeric powder
2 bay leaves
*3 pieces of cinnamon, 4 cardamoms, 4 cloves for whole garom
mashla*
2 teaspoons of sugar
500 ml (16 fl oz) of water
2 teaspoons of flour
Salt and sugar to taste

If the oil in which you have fried the fishballs has been reduced too much, you can add some fresh oil to it and heat it. Then throw in the bay leaves and garom mashla, fry for a couple of minutes, add the onions and fry till golden brown. Add 2 teaspoons of sugar and wait till it turns to a caramel colour, after which add the other spices. Fry these well, add the water and salt as needed. When it comes to the boil, add the fishballs and keep covered for five to six minutes. Taste for salt, add flour to thicken the gravy and remove. Once again, you can use less or more water, depending on how much gravy you would like, and the spices will have to be adjusted accordingly. This, too, can be garnished with coriander leaves. Or you can mix in a small handful of fresh chopped mint to the fish mixture before making the fishballs.

6
CROSSING THE BORDERS

After college, when I got the opportunity to pursue graduate studies in the United States, I was overjoyed. My parents did not try to stop me, but fear, anxiety, and a sense of desolation lay very close to the surface. The anxiety was particularly intense because I was the first girl in the family to go off alone, unmarried, to a distant country. Like all heedless young people eager for adventure and independence, I ignored all signs of this, until one day my grandmother asked if I didn't feel sad at the thought of leaving behind everything I knew and loved. I was stricken with guilt and sorrow, but it was also a moment of revelation. I saw how far I had moved from my moorings, how ready I was to let go.

My parents must have consoled themselves with thoughts of my future success, expecting the daughter to return in a few years and settle down to a productive and predictable life in her hometown. But within a year of my arrival in the United States, I dashed all those hopes to the ground with the catastrophic announcement that I was going to marry a Bengali Muslim from East Pakistan (now Bangladesh) whom I had met as a fellow student.

Looking back after so many years, I can clearly imagine the echoing bewilderment that must have filled both my parents' home and the house of my childhood where my widowed grandmother still lived with some of her married sons. How can she even dream of it, they must have said, how can she possibly go and spend her life with this man in a Muslim country? Doesn't she know our history, of the centuries of hatred between Hindus and Muslims in India, of what happened during Partition in 1947—all those riots, rapes, and massacres? Is she bewitched? Hasn't she read about how women are treated in Muslim countries, doesn't she know she'll lose all the freedom she's so used to? Hasn't she heard of Muslim men being permitted to have four wives? And (above all) how can she reject all our traditions of worship? Won't a Muslim husband force her to convert to Islam? Surely she must have gone mad. Or this man has put a spell on her. And on the food front—won't they force her to eat beef, violating the norms of Hindu belief in the sacredness of the cow? Added to this was the shame of having to confess to social peers and relatives that a daughter of the house had violated all the taboos.

In as many ways as possible, parents and relatives tried to dissuade me from stepping beyond the point of no return. An amazing fear and revulsion of Muslims, a community that I hadn't personally encountered much in Calcutta, leapt from the pages of letters. But I remained adamant. My family, I felt, was showing me an aspect that was entirely unfamiliar. My upbringing had indeed been remarkably free of expressions of sectarian hatred by any of my relatives. Obviously, as I now realized, those prejudices were ingrained below the surface and were welling out now, as they feared for my happiness and dreaded their own impending social disgrace.

It's hard to say who felt more betrayed, my family or I. In my unsubtle, immature anger, I found it unforgivable that neither intelligence nor education had freed them from petty parochialism. I also raged at the layers of hypocrisy that I felt were now being exposed. For although we were orthodox brahmans by caste, we belonged to the Vaishnava sect. One of the tenets of Vaishnava reformism (which began as the Bhakti Movement in Bengal in the fifteenth century) was that birth and caste did not matter, that we were all equals before the Lord.

We never resolved our differences. Against their wishes, I married, and after a few years, left the United States and went to live in the newly created, war-ravaged country of

Bangladesh. En route, we stopped in Calcutta to make an uneasy peace with my family. Almost everyone loaded me with guilt and blame, although nothing was said directly nor was my husband treated with any overt incivility. But my devout grandmother defied all expectations by welcoming the heathen outsider with open arms. During our stay in Calcutta, we visited her often, and I was amazed, delighted, and utterly comforted to see the ease with which she became a narrator again, holding him transfixed in her web of magic myths about Krishna, Radha, gods, demons, and others. What's more, when she presented my husband with post-ritual offerings of fruits and sweets, he, an atheist, accepted with alacrity. Watching them together, I felt it was a triumph of the narrator and the worshipper.

In Bangladesh, it was my turn to be the outsider. This newborn country that was only a forty-minute plane ride from the city of my birth, where people spoke my language and looked and dressed like me, constantly presented unfamiliar facets to well-known things. The food I ate during our initial stay in my in-laws' house was apparently the same rice, dal, vegetables, and fish that I had grown up on, and yet everything tasted different, though no less delicious. It took me a while to figure out that the one ubiquitous element in these dishes was onions—an ingredient that was used in our household only for cooking meat (goatmeat or chicken) and occasionally combined with lentils and potatoes. My grandparents, in fact, never ate chicken, a 'heathen' bird associated with Muslims, like the onion itself. One of my uncles had broken that household taboo and introduced his siblings to chicken, but never my grandparents. As for the numerous greens and vegetables available in our lush tropical region, they were only rarely combined with onions in my family's kitchen. But my Muslim in-laws and friends wouldn't dream of preparing them without throwing in a handful of sliced onion. No vegetable—greens, gourds, potatoes, cauliflowers, cabbage—escaped the ubiquitous onion. Nor did any kind of fish. This allium, it seemed, was an inevitable ingredient here, like salt.

Contrary to my family's apprehensions, my in-laws spared me any pressure to convert to Islam. But I could not remain unaware of the daily religious reality of this new home. No tinkling bells or resounding conch shells from temples and houses, but the song of the muezzin sounding from minarets, calling the faithful to prayer five times a day; no aesthetic rituals with flower, leaf, and perfume, but austere obeisance on a prayer rug before an invisible god; no bustling, tumultuous crowds of men and women in temples crushing forward to make their offerings before an image and receive sacrament from the priest, but orderly, all-male prayer assemblies in mosques. God in this Muslim universe had no humanly definable shape or form; the concept of incarnations was absurd, any thought of offering him food every day and then partaking of it unimaginable.

The only time that food played a part in worship was at the great festival of Bakr-id, which commemorated the Old Testament tale of Abraham's readiness to sacrifice his son to the Lord. In the city of Dhaka where we lived, the affluent (including our landlord) bought goats and cows and offered them for *korbani*, or sacrifice. The animals were slaughtered with the recommended two-and-a-half strokes of the knife across the throat. The rivers of blood ran and ran, flowing down porch steps, into the courtyards, and draining into sewer pipes. For a true Muslim, no meat is halal or sanctioned, unless the slaughtering is done right and the blood drained out completely. The ferrous smell of blood rose up to the sky as kites and crows shrieked overhead. Expert butchers, hired for the occasion, cut and portioned the meat, while servants made packages under directions from their masters. The beauty of Bakr-Id lies in the injunction of sharing the meat one has offered as sacrifice—with family, friends, and the poor. As the day progressed, I noticed hordes of beggars lined up outside the ample, walled houses, clamouring for their share.

That first experience of Bakr-Id was shocking. I had never seen animal sacrifice before, although some Hindu sects do have a tradition of making animal sacrifices, especially those who are followers of the goddess Kali. Although my family was not vegetarian, meat was eaten only on special occasions and we were shielded from the blood and gore since slaughterhouses were far from markets. On this Bakr-Id afternoon, when the gift packages of meat from in-laws and friends started to arrive at our house, I was initially repelled. Quickly, I gave away most of the meat to the servants. But on second thoughts, I decided to have the last remaining portion prepared in the slow-cooking method that is traditionally used for korbani meat. I knew I could never belong to this community through faith, fast, or prayer. But perhaps eating could be one way of participating. Perhaps, I also hoped, it would help me feel less of an outsider.

But inclusion is not so easy. Friendships formed and filled my heart with delight, only to be tarnished by small manifestations of distrust towards me as the Hindu woman from across the border. As in the case of the United States and Mexico, the prevailing paranoia of a small nation obligated to a big neighbour (the Indian army had helped liberate Bangladesh in 1971 from the occupying Pakistani forces) must have coloured many people's reactions towards me. Anything I took for granted would suddenly seem to waver like a reflection in moving waters.

Those were tough times to live through—for me, for the land, for its people. The days were filled with news and evidence of famine, floods, inflation, anarchy, and betrayal. Heavy, fly-blown heat, the dankness of unremitting rain, the constant cries of people begging for food, the insecurity of existence, unending stories about corruption, abuse of power, and mounting lawlessness—all contributed to the sensation of being wrapped in a miasma of despair. As I struggled to make sense of my life in a landscape of extraordinary suffering, nothing was farther from my mind than the smell of sandalwood paste, the taste of ritual offerings, or evenings of kirtan-singing in a Hindu household in Calcutta.

But Krishna and his offerings were not to be forgotten so easily.

One oppressive afternoon in late August, I found myself, along with some colleagues, in a remote Bangladeshi village, conducting a drinking water survey for an international aid agency. It was the month of Bhadra according to the Bengali calendar, a time when the monsoon starts withdrawing from Bengal, leaving land and air infused with an oppressive, glowering humidity, panting for the dryness of autumn and winter. In the medieval kirtan lyrics, it is the month of despair— when the beautiful milkmaid Radha bemoans the absence of Krishna, who has abandoned her and gone off to reclaim his kingly destiny.

We, too, were on the verge of despair. Everything seemed to have gone wrong on this trip. Buses, ferries, and boats had all played havoc with our foolishly optimistic schedules. In the dead of afternoon, we stood forlorn in the middle of a desolate, sun-parched village, wondering if any reprieve could be found from the ungodly heat. We were dying for something to drink, a bit of shade to rest in till some alternative transport could be found. Neither seemed within the realm of possibility until a ragged boy appeared from nowhere and asked if we wanted some tea.

Silently, we followed him down a lumpy, packed-earth road to a rudimentary shelter of canvas supported by bamboos planted in the ground. Underneath were two rickety benches, one raised on bricks to serve as a table. A sooty kettle sat atop a primitive, wood-fired stove, near which a thin, bare-chested man, wearing the traditional lungi, was pouring tea from another kettle into chipped earthen cups. He looked at us with a friendly grin composed of only three teeth and waved toward the bench. As we lowered ourselves onto it with palpable relief, the man handed the cups to the boy who carefully put each one down in front of us. Our silence must have underscored our bone-deep weariness. For the man decided that these city slickers needed more than tea. Squatting down, he opened a large tin that sat beside the stove and began to take out handfuls of something, putting them in a battered enamel bowl.

Biscuits for tea, I thought hopefully. Then the boy came forward and put the bowl down in front of us, and I saw what the pastel-brown objects were. Batashas.

The smell of much-brewed tea and steamed milk, framed by the odour of sweaty bodies, dried cowdung, and burning firewood, all retreated before a surging memory of sandalwood paste, incense smoke, and oil burning in a lamp with a cotton wick. As I had done so often in that other world, I put out my hand and let the fragility of a batasha fill the hollow of my palm. I placed it in my mouth and bit into it, letting it dissolve into a pool of mild, refreshing sweetness. A charge of energy pulsed through my body. For one moment, I felt the pall of inertia, doubt, and despair lift away from me. In this alien land so perversely close to my home, I found myself once again ready and eager, sharply poised to give chase, filled with the confidence of capturing Krishna's largesse.

As time went by, I was to discover the distinctiveness, delicacy, and variety of the food cooked by Bangladeshis. True to Muslim tradition, their preparations of chicken, *khashi* (castrated goat), duck, and beef were infinitely superior to anything I had tasted in Hindu homes. That was only to be expected. Muslims were supposed to be wizards with meat. But what served as a revelation was the conjunction of unexpected, unrelated elements, resulting in gustatory experiences of unprecedented delight. Poppy seed paste, which I had grown to consider a common and very appropriate accompaniment for delicate vegetables like *jhinge* (similar in taste and consistency to courgettes or marrows), was boldly added to chicken and lamb. The *Khashir rezala*, a glorious Muslim invention which I had also tasted in restaurants in India, exploded with a sudden novel piquancy in my mouth as I tasted the sauce that included yogurt, lemon, *kewra* (extracted from the screwpine flower), enhanced with the zestiness of ripened green chillies. The koi, a freshwater perch much prized in Bengal, was combined with oranges to become an eclectic pleasure.

On a winter evening, I found myself the guest of honour in a rural homestead. My hostess and her daughters were busy tending the food that was being cooked over wood fires burning in deep pits dug into the earth. That meal of freshly caught carp seasoned with green chillies and green coriander, duck nestling in a rich sauce flavoured with coconut milk, and stacks of paper-thin chapattis made out of freshly ground rice flour was not only ambrosial to my taste buds, but also a severe lesson in humility. No preconceived notions of superiority as an urban, educated, sophisticated or well-travelled person could survive in the face of such culinary perfection.

Those rice flour chapattis took on a very different aspect when I saw them being served in town during the great Islamic festival of Shab-e-barat. Custom in Bangladesh decrees that the occasion should be celebrated by eating rice flour chapattis with an array of *haluas*. Europeans and Americans know the term as halvah, a Middle Eastern concoction. In the Indian subcontinent it has come to mean a dish made of finely ground grains or legumes sautéed in ghee, flavoured with whole sweet spices like cinnamon or cardamom, and sweetened with sugar, not honey or molasses. The commonest variety is made with cream of wheat. But during my first Shab-e-barat, I was dumbfounded to see an amazing variety of haluas, made with ingredients like plain white flour, split pea flour, gluten, eggs, nuts, white gourd, carrots, and yes, even meat.

Perhaps my most memorable lesson in the power food has to upset preconceived ideas came to me through fish—the darling of the Bengali palate, whether Ghoti or Bangal, Hindu or Muslim. And of all the myriad species that the region is blessed with, the undisputed king is the hilsa, called *ilish* in Bengal. A large anadromous fish, like the American shad, the hilsa spawns during the monsoon in estuarine waters and then travels upstream through Bengal to northern India. Its unique flavour, soft, rich flesh, delicate roe, and graceful appearance cause Bengalis to swoon with appreciation. Even its plentiful bones cannot detract from its appeal.

Before coming to Bangladesh, I had eaten hilsa cooked in a variety of ways, including the classic preparation of *ilish paturi* (pieces of fish coated in mustard oil and ground mustard, wrapped in banana leaves, and cooked in a slow oven). Over the centuries, Ghotis and Bangals have come up with many different ways to cook this delightful fish. Even the British in India made one of their few culinary contributions in the form of smoked hilsa. Two experiences with this fish have taught me about unity and diversity in Bengal's food practices.

Ghotis and Bangals in West Bengal have traditionally engaged in jocular rivalry about the taste and quality of hilsa from the two main rivers, Ganga (West Bengal) and Padma (East Bengal). Cooking styles have also been the source of friendly rivalry. But one of the things that we Ghotis always shuddered over was the strange pre-cooking practice of the Bangals. Since the fish is always bought whole, cleaning and cutting is mostly done at home. Any other fish is carefully washed after it has been cut up into pieces. Blood and slime are repulsive to Bengalis and must be thoroughly removed. With the hilsa, however, the Hindus of East Bengal seem to have lost their heads. So eager are they to preserve the fish's unique flavour and taste, that they refuse to wash the blood from the pieces before cooking!

Had anybody asked me when I went to Bangladesh whether I would encounter a similar practice there (after all, this really was East Bengal, land of the Bangals), I would have given a definite no. For I knew that in Islam, blood is haram, an abomination. Imagine my astonishment when I found the mother of a Bangladeshi Muslim friend, preparing to cook hilsa for our lunch, refusing to wash off the blood on the same grounds I had heard years ago in Calcutta—all the taste will be washed away. I admit I felt very queasy as I ate the fish, but I did relish discovering this commonality that had transcended religious barriers.

The second lesson from hilsa brings me back to the matter of preconceived notions and irrational prejudices. Fish in Bengal is always cooked with our preferred medium, mustard oil, which has a pungency that nicely balances fishy odours. In the absence of mustard oil, other vegetable oils, such as canola, peanut, or soybean oil, are used. Hilsa lends itself particularly to the flavour of mustard. Not only the oil, but freshly ground mustard is frequently used in its preparation because the pungency cuts the fattiness of the hilsa. The fish can also be combined with sour tastes like that of tamarind or *karamcha* berries, or with spices like cumin, coriander and ground red chillies. But never could I imagine hilsa with ghee, onions, coconut milk, lemon, and yes, even sugar. Never, that is, until a cook who worked in my house in Bangladesh declared he was going to treat me to a very special dish. When I heard what had gone into its preparation, I was dumbfounded. Hilsa and ghee—heresy! Hilsa with onions and coconut milk—blasphemy! But of course it is the tongue that is the ultimate arbiter, and one mouthful convinced me that my food universe would be singularly diminished if this dish did not become part of it.

It has been many years since that revelation. I am happy to say that I have personally made this dish for family and friends in Calcutta and have been gratified by their incredulous appreciation. And with each attempt, I have realized afresh how environment and historical circumstance load us with the baggage of suspicion and prejudice. An onion—that same allium which surprised me so often in Bangladesh—whose top layers are decaying from disuse can be the perfect metaphor for such a state of mind. For I believe that if we make an effort to peel away the layers, and reach the centre, most of us can find a core that is fresh and untouched, waiting to be inscribed with new ideas.

KHASHIR REZALA

FOR EIGHT PEOPLE

INGREDIENTS

2 kg (4 lb) of meat
250 gm (8 oz) of grated onion
2 tablespoons of ground ginger
3 teaspoons of ground garlic
5-6 whole cardamoms
5-6 pieces of cinnamon 2.5 cm (1 in) long
250 gm (8 oz) of yoghurt
1 tablespoon of sugar
3 teaspoons of salt
250 ml (8 fl oz) of ghee
250 ml (8 fl oz) of warm whole milk
A tiny pinch of saffron
20 whole green chillies

METHOD

For eight people, take 2 kg (4 lb) of meat, cubed and washed, to make the Khashir rezala. Combine this in a large pot with onion, ginger, garlic, cardamom, cinnamon, yoghurt, sugar, salt and ghee. Once all of this is thoroughly mixed, cover the pot and let it cook on a low flame for about half an hour. Then uncover and stir the meat well and cover again. Leave on the stove till all the moisture has evaporated and the ghee has risen to the surface. Next take some warm whole milk, add saffron to it, and pour it over the meat. Add the green chillies, reduce heat to simmer and leave the meat tightly covered for another half an hour before it is ready to serve. Some cooks select ripened chillies (fresh, not dried) for this recipe. The red colour stands out in a most pleasing contrast against the pale yellow of the gravy.

ILISH PATURI

INGREDIENTS

500 gm (1 lb) of hilsa peti
½ teaspoon of turmeric powder
2 tablespoons of ground mustard
Green chillies
2 tablespoons of mustard oil
Salt to taste

METHOD

For this ilish paturi, take the fish pieces, clean them and mix them thoroughly with salt, turmeric, the ground mustard, green chillies and a liberal helping of mustard oil. The whole mixture is then wrapped in banana leaves and the packet tied with string before it is thrust among the dying embers of a clay oven, or toasted on a tawa or flat pan over a low heat. The packet is turned over several times. By the time the top layer of leaf is burnt black, the fish should be ready. The process can also be duplicated in an oven set at 150°C (300°F, Gas mark 1). In the absence of banana leaves, aluminium foil can be used. Once the fish is cooked, it should be removed from the wrappings and all the sauce scraped out with a spoon. The moisture and oil from the fish combined with the mustard paste and oil will produce quite a bit of gravy.

7

THE BONTI OF BENGAL

In the days when most Bengalis lived in extended, multi-generational families, women had to make large meals every day. Usually the elderly grandmother or widowed aunt was responsible for cutting the vegetables, while the younger women took on the more arduous task of cooking over the hot stove. This ritual of cutting, called *kutno kota*, was almost as important as the daily rituals carried out for the household gods.

In the kitchens of the west, the cook stands at a table or counter and uses a knife. But mention a kitchen to a Bengali, or evoke a favourite dish, and more often than not the image that comes to mind will be of a woman seated on the floor, cutting, chopping, or cooking. In the Indian subcontinent, especially in Bengal, this is the typical posture. For centuries, the Bengali cook and her assistant have remained firmly grounded on the floor, a tradition reflecting the paucity of furniture inside the house. A bed for both sleeping and sitting was usually the most important piece of furniture, but outside the bedroom people sat or rested on mats spread out on the floor, or on squares of rug called asans. In the kitchen they often sat on small rectangular or square wooden platforms called piris or jalchoukis, which raised them an inch or two above the floor.

From this closeness to the earth evolved the practice of sitting down both to prepare and to cook food. Enter the bonti, a protean cutting instrument on which generations of Bengali women have learned to peel, chop, dice, and shred. Despite the recent incursion of knives, peelers, graters, and other modern, western-style kitchen utensils, the bonti is still alive and well in the rural and urban kitchens of Bengal.

Some of my fondest childhood memories involve sitting near my grandmother as she peeled and sliced the vegetables for the day's main afternoon meal. A grand array of shapes and colours surrounded her as she sat at the bonti: purple and greenish-white eggplants, green-and-white striped *patols* (a favourite gourd-like vegetable), the leafy green of the *noteshaak* with their fleshy, rhubarb-like stems, yellow crescents of pumpkin, pale-skinned potatoes. During holidays and school vacations I always sat and watched . . .

My grandmother takes a long, purple eggplant and dexterously halves it against the blade, then starts cutting one of the halves into smaller pieces. I pick up the remaining half and inspect the white, seed-studded flesh. Something is moving. A worm, secretly embedded in the flesh, is now forced into the open. What is it, I ask, what is that worm called, how did it get inside when there were no wormholes on the outside? And she launches into a story from the Mahabharata, about a king who sought to protect himself from the vengeful lord of the snakes by building a palace on top of a glass column and sealing it tight. But one day, as he bit into a ripe rosy-gold mango, a tiny worm came out and bit him in the arm. The king felt the agony of the most potent venom race through his blood and before he fainted, saw the worm transformed into a majestic serpent. She smiles at me, takes the eggplant from my hands and cuts off the infested portion. I look at the crawling worm in the discarded bit of eggplant with new respect . . .

A Bengali lexicon compiled by Jnanendramohan Das (*Bangla Bhashar Abhidhan*) reveals that although the term bonti has been in the Bengali language for many years, it actually derives from the language of the ancient tribal inhabitants of the eastern regions of the subcontinent. Das traces the word bonti back to ancient Bengali narrative poems, such as Ghanaram Chakrabarti's poem *Dharmamangal*, composed during the reign of Dharma Pal (775-810 AD), the second ruler of Bengal's Pal Dynasty. In his definitive history of Bengal, *Bangalir Itihash*, the historian Niharranjan Ray presents compelling evidence of the indigenous people who settled in Bengal long before the Aryans came to India, and whose language, customs, and ritualistic beliefs still permeate the cultural life of Bengal. Ray also notes that Buddhist terracotta sculptures from the days of the Pal dynasty depict people using the bonti blade to cut and portion fish.

Basically, the bonti is a curved blade rising out of a narrow, flat, wooden base. Sometimes the blade is mounted on a small iron tripod to increase its height. Its versatility lies in the many different types and sizes of both blade and base, as well as from the various uses to which it is put. The bonti's uniqueness comes from the posture required to use it: one must either squat on one's haunches or sit on the floor with one knee raised while the corresponding foot presses down on the base. As in other 'floor-oriented' cultures, such as Japan, the people of Bengal were accustomed to squatting or sitting on the floor for indefinite periods of time. An 1832 volume by Mrs S. C. Belnos, *Twenty-four Plates Illustrative of Hindoo and European Manners in Bengal*, depicts a Bengali kitchen complete with utensils and a woman seated in front of a low stove, cooking. The author comments: 'Their furniture consists of low beds, small stools, a chest or two, perhaps an old-fashioned chair on which the master sits with his legs crossed under him, a Hookah of cocanut [*sic*] shell on a brass stand . . .' Even today in rural Bengal, people— especially men—squat comfortably on porches or under large shade trees as they smoke and chat. Only after the European presence was well established later in the nineteenth century did the living room or dining room equipped with couches, chairs, and tables become part of the Bengali home.

The bonti also appears in Kalighat paintings, a body of indigenous works produced in the vicinity of the Kalighat Temple, built in 1829 on the banks of the river Hooghly in Calcutta. As Calcutta grew under British rule and its Bengali residents developed a 'babu' culture, the Kalighat painters focused their attention on urban, rather than rural, life. One of these paintings shows a woman cutting a whole fish, possibly a carp, on a bonti.

To use a knife of any size or shape, the cook must bear down with one hand on the item being cut, at the same time holding the food with the other hand to prevent it from slipping. But unlike the knife, the bonti uses horizontal, rather than vertical, force. The cook positions herself in front of the tool, one foot pressed firmly against the wooden base. She then uses both hands to slide the vegetable, fruit, fish, or meat against the curving blade that faces her. To those used to working with a knife, the delicacy with which the rigidly-positioned blade cuts seems miraculous: it peels the tiniest potato, trims the tendrils from string beans, splits the fleshy stems of plants, chops greens into minute particles for stir-frying, and even scales the largest fish. At the great fish markets, as in Calcutta, fishmongers sit tightly packed as they dismember giant carp and hilsa on huge, gleaming bontis, all the while engaging in jocular repartee about who has the better fish.

Like knives, bontis come in many different sizes, with blades varying in height, width, and shape. Women using the instrument at home generally have two medium-sized bontis, one for cutting vegetables, the other for fish and meat (collectively known as *amish*). This separation of vegetarian and non-vegetarian food was rigidly practised in all traditional Hindu homes until fairly recently and led to the term *ansh-bonti* for the tools used to cut fish or meat (ansh means 'fish scale').

Professional cooks dealing with large volumes of food use considerably sturdier bontis than the housewives. Their ansh-bontis had to be strong enough to cut a twenty- or thirty-pound carp, the blades proportionately wider and higher. The bonti blade is generally made of iron rather than stainless steel, and it tends to rust if not immediately dried. Repeated use blunts the blade, so itinerant experts roam the cities with special equipment for sharpening bontis and knives.

An interesting variant is the *kuruni*, used for the specific purpose of grating coconuts. In this type of bonti, the blade curves out of the wooden base in the usual way, but its tip is crowned with a round serrated piece of metal. The cook sits in front of the kuruni with the front end of its base on a woven mat or tray, or even on a piece of newspaper. Holding one half of a fresh coconut in both hands, she scrapes it with circular motions against the metal disk as the coconut flesh rains down in a gentle stream of white.

Such are the day-to-day uses of the bonti in the Bengali kitchen. But as with any implement with a long history, this tool is endowed with a wealth of associations reaching far beyond the mundane. Although professional male cooks use the bonti, it is inextricably associated with Bengali women, and the image of a woman seated at her bonti, surrounded by baskets of vegetables, is a cultural icon. Holding the vegetable or fish or meat in both hands and running it into the blade makes the act of cutting a relatively softer, gentler motion than the more masculine gesture of bringing a knife down with force on a hard surface: the food is embraced even as it is dismembered.

The woman at the bonti is not always an elderly storyteller like my grandmother. The young, nubile daughter of the family or the newly married bride at the bonti are also part of Bengali iconography. As she joyfully manipulates food against the versatile blade, the young woman epitomizes feminine abilities. When marriages were arranged in rural Bengal, the bridegroom's family would come to look over the prospective bride, asking to see her kitchen skills and noting how skilfully she could use the bonti. In the southern district of Barisal in Bangladesh, it was not enough for a prospective bride to chop just any vegetable. Her future in-laws often demanded that she sit at the bonti and cut a bunch of *kalaishaak*, the leafy greens of the legume *khesari dal*, whose fibrous leaves and stems have to be chopped very fine before stir-frying. The ideal bride had to be able to reduce the resistant bunch into minute particles of green. Handling the bonti well had another advantage in Barisal. The local women used their bontis to defend themselves and their homes against gangs of armed robbers who attacked prosperous homesteads when the men were away.

Bengali literature contains many references to another, less domestic aspect of the woman at the bonti. Recurring images portray her as young and demure, sitting with her head bent, concentrating on her hands as she moves the vegetable or fish towards the lethal blade. Often a married woman is pictured, her head modestly covered with the end of her sari, whose colourful border frames her face and hair. But the discreet posture and modest covering are a foil for a flirtatious element in extended-family life, which offers virtually no privacy. A man—whether a husband or a romantic interest—can expect many eloquent, sidelong glances cast with surreptitious turns of the head as the woman goes about her domestic tasks with the bonti.

An extension of this mild titillation is found in *Shobha*, a fascinating album of photographs by Gurudas Chattopadhyay, published around 1930. His photographs portray some of Calcutta's best-known prostitutes and are obviously intended for erotic stimulation. But this is no collection of *Playboy*-like nudes. Instead, each woman has been photographed fully clothed and seated before a bonti! Here is a study in body language: the straight back, the parted legs (one crossed, the other raised), the coy eyes peeking out from under the sari covering the head. To the Bengali viewer/voyeur of the time, the bonti, by enforcing this posture, created a uniquely erotic vision of the female figure, rich in suggestiveness.

Despite its long history, it is probably inevitable that in the new global century the bonti will eventually vanish. The kitchens of Bengal are rapidly changing. Knives rather than bontis are becoming the cutting implements of choice. Tables and countertops are triumphing over the floor; chairs, tables, and couches are becoming as integral to the home as its doors and windows. Women no longer live in extended families, nor do their mornings consist of the leisurely ritual of kutno kota, when several women worked together, forming a sisterhood of the bonti. Now women are likely to work outside the home, which leaves little time for that kind of domestic fellowship. But for those of us who remember, the bonti will continue to be part of a woman's kitchen life.

8

FIVE LITTLE SEEDS

Several years ago, when I spent some time in London, I used to visit a Bengali friend who lived on the top floor of an apartment building tenanted by people from different parts of the world. Though I never saw any of them, their typical cooking odours clearly demarcated their home territories. As I entered the front door and climbed the stairs, I inhaled my way through Britain on the first floor (corned beef and boiled cabbage), China on the second (soya sauce, garlic, and Szechwan peppercorns), Italy on the third (tomato, basil, garlic), and finally to Bengal, where my friend's delicate yet aromatic concoctions (*chachchari*, a dry, spicy mixed vegetable dish, roasted *moong dal*, tamarind fish) originated.

In America, where I now live, cooking odours can still provide a key to the ethnic identity of households in urban neighbourhoods. This is especially true of large cities where immigrants from many countries live side by side. I have often heard people identify the fragrance of cinnamon, cardamom and clove, especially in conjunction with onion and garlic, as 'Indian' cooking. That there is no such thing as 'Indian' cooking, that each region has its distinctive culinary identity, is a point that escapes most outsiders.

To me, the signature aroma of Bengal is panchphoron, a five-spice mixture that is the building block of many of our favourite dishes. Unlike the Chinese five-spice mixture which is generally sold in powdered form, the Bengali panchphoron is made up of whole spices—equal portions of cumin, nigella, fennel, fenugreek, and mustard. Native to either Asia or Europe, each of these spices has played an important role in the cuisines of many races and regions. But only Bengalis seem to have come up with the idea of combining them as a unique flavouring agent. They generally use panchphoron as the first step in cooking a dish. A pinch thrown into hot oil—especially the pungent mustard oil that is traditionally used in Bengal—will immediately release a unique aroma, sharp yet delicate. Panch means five in Bengali (as in Hindi) and phoron comes from the Sanskrit *sphoton*, which implies a kind of outburst. In this case, it is the outburst of flavour that accompanies the spices sputtering in the hot oil. Dried or fresh chillies usually accompany panchphoron into the pot. As the cooking progresses, other ground spices may also be added to some dishes flavoured with panchphoron.

Intrigued by the unique Bengali usage of the spices constituting panchphoron, I tried to learn more about them. Some, I found, have a long history. References to cumin—*Cumin cyminum*—for instance, can be found in the Bible. The collection of ancient Roman recipes, *Apicius*, indicates its widespread use by the Romans. Pliny, writing in the first century A.D., praised cumin for its enlivening quality. Today, cumin is used not only in the food of India, but also that of Afghanistan, Iran, and even Mexico. However, the seed referred to as *kalojeera* (a literal translation being black cumin but called nigella in English) in Bengal has produced endless confusion in translation. It neither resembles cumin in taste nor are the two botanically related. Some people also translate it as black caraway or black sesame. Native to the countries bordering the eastern Mediterranean, black cumin is small, wedge-shaped, and, naturally, black. But when added to hot oil, it releases a pungent odour very similar to that of onion. Hence another misnomer—onion seed!

Of the two 'f's that belong to panchphoron, fennel and fenugreek, the former (*Foeniculum vulgare*) is well known in the west. This plant of the parsley family is native to southern Europe and was carried by Arab traders all over the Middle East and to India. Patrons of Indian restaurants in the west are well aware of the Indian practice of chewing fennel seeds after a meal as a breath freshener. But the practice is also rooted in the well-demonstrated value of fennel as an aid to digestion. In a tropical climate like that of India, fennel is also considered to have a cooling effect on the body. Fenugreek (*Trigonella foenumgraecum*), on the other hand, needs to be treated with extreme caution. A little overheating can turn it extremely bitter. The plant's botanical name means 'Greek hay', and it is native to southern Europe and Asia. Its leaves are rich in vitamins and sugar and cooked like other edible greens.

The fifth ingredient in panchphoron is mustard, the brown Indian variety (*Brassica juncea*) which is sometimes called Chinese mustard. Aside from providing cooking oil, mustard is an important spice in Bengali cuisine. Whole mustard seeds are added to the hot oil as a flavouring agent in some dishes, while the pungency of ground mustard is the basis of many famous Bengali fish preparations, notably *shorshe-ilish*. As a child, I was always intrigued by the folk belief that mustard could chase away ghosts. Despite its potency, however, the presence of mustard in panchphoron is rather muted, suborned by the combined flavours of fenugreek, cumin, and nigella.

It is impossible to determine how or when the Bengalis came up with the magic formula of combining these five disparate elements into a single flavour-package. But it is reasonable to assume that its use is correlated to a style of cooking that is more delicate than that of northern India, depending as it does on heightened flavours rather than heavy spices. Interestingly, it is the Hindus of Bengal, not the Muslims, who tend to make prolific use of panchphoron. This is possibly because of the emphasis on vegetarian cooking among the Bengali Hindus, especially widows, who were forbidden any fish, flesh, or egg. Bengali Hindu cooks seem to think that almost any item of food can benefit from the addition of panchphoron.

The simplest application is in vegetable stir-fries. Once the hot oil is impregnated with the aroma of the five seeds and dried red chillies, vegetables like spinach, eggplant, thinly-sliced potatoes, string beans can be thrown in, sautéd with a little salt, and kept covered over medium heat until the natural juices have emerged, mingled, and evaporated. Served at the beginning of a traditional Bengali meal, this kind of dish helps prepare the palate for the more complex vegetable preparations like *chachchari* or *ghanto*, which may start with the addition of panchphoron or some other flavouring to the oil, but may then be enriched with ground spices like fresh ginger, cumin, coriander, turmeric, and chilli powder.

And in a fish-loving region like Bengal, this signature spice mixture has also lent its delicate yet unmistakable aroma to the numerous fish dishes that Bengalis are known for. The traditional midday meal usually has to include a fish jhol (a thin flavourful gravy) or a fish *jhal* (a hot and spicy sauce that coats the fish). In both of these, panchphoron can play a vital flavouring role. During the height of the summer, Bengalis often make fish into *ambol* or *tauk*—a sour and spicy sauce that often includes tamarind. While some cooks flavour the oil for ambol solely with mustard, others resort to the versatile panchphoron.

One of my most-remembered fragrances is that of roasted panchphoron, which was then crushed into powder to be added to the numerous pickles and chutneys that were made during the summer. My favourite was green mango pickle. Enormous glass jars full of the spice-coated mango quarters submerged in dark yellow mustard oil sat sunning themselves on the balcony. It was forbidden food for us children. But aided by my younger cousin Benu (who visited us each summer from Delhi), I was often bold enough to risk discovery and sneak a few pieces from the pickle jar when the adults were taking their afternoon naps. Oh, the pleasure of sitting on the polished balcony floor heated by the sun, legs stretched out, back against the wall, and slowly savouring the spicy tartness of those forbidden pickles, all the while keeping one ear open for the sound of approaching footsteps.

The sound and aroma of these five seeds meeting hot oil are now resurrected for me only when I am using panchphoron for cooking or when I am visiting another Bengali cook. Their absence from my day-to-day reality seems, to me, a perfect metaphor of the distance that now intervenes between my origins and myself. Like many members of a diaspora, I wonder how the accumulated weight of that distance will eventually affect my memory of what was once so real, so inescapable. Houses and apartments in this country are designed to enclose, to hold in heat, smell, and other emanations and only the strongest of odours—onion and garlic, fish and meat—tend to escape. I no longer have the opportunity of laughing, as I did during my childhood in Bengal, at the series of hefty sneezes with which our neighbour across the street greeted the odour of panchphoron and dried chillies wafting on the breeze from our kitchen almost every day. There may be some comfort in the privacy afforded by the enclosed living spaces we now inhabit in the West, but a reduction of the community awareness of the small details of each other's lives also means a lessening of the human connection.

NARKEL ALOOR CHACHHARI
INGREDIENTS
1 small ripe coconut

500 gram potatoes

1/3 cup oil (preferably mustard oil)

1½ teaspoon turmeric powder

4 or 5 green chillies, split lengthwise
1 teaspoon panch phoron
Salt and sugar to taste

METHOD

Split the coconut in half, discard the water and grind the flesh on a coconut grater.

Cut the potatoes into small cubes and wash well.

Heat the oil in a karai, throw in the panch phoron and green chillies. When the seeds sputter and both chillies and panch phoron have released their fragrance, add the potatoes. Stir vigorously until the potatoes start to become golden brown. Sprinkle half a cup of water over them, to keep them from burning or sticking. Add the grated coconut, turmeric, salt and a bit of sugar, stir well and cover tightly. Reduce the heat to medium-low. Check from time to time. If necessary, sprinkle small amounts of water over the potatoes and stir. Once the potatoes are done, raise the heat to high, stir well until the dish achieves a toasty colour and consistency. Check for salt and sugar (the chachhari should have a sweet undertaste) and remove from the stove.

Serve with rice or luchi.

BHAJA MUGER DAL

INGREDIENTS

1 cup yellow moong dal
1 teaspoon whole cumin seeds
4 bay leaves
4 green chillies
1 tablespoon freshly chopped ginger
2 ½ teaspoons ghee (clarified butter)
Salt and sugar to taste

METHOD

Dry-roast the moong dal in a karai. Start over high heat, and then reduce heat to medium after three minutes. Stir constantly for a total of about seven or eight minutes, or until the pale yellow of the moong dal has turned medium brown and gives off a nutty aroma.

Remove the dal and wash thoroughly in cold water, rinsing several times to get rid of any dust and impurities.

In a thick-bottomed pan, bring to boil three cups of water and add the washed dal to it. Bring to boil again, reduce heat to a simmer, and leave covered for about half an hour.

Check to see if the dal grains are soft and blend thoroughly, using an eggbeater. You can add more water if you want to liquefy the consistency. Add salt and sugar and taste. The sweetness should be perceptible.

In a karai, heat the ghee, bay leaves, and cumin seeds. When the seeds start sputtering and release their aroma, add the chopped ginger and green chillies. Stir-fry for a minute or two, and pour in the cooked dal very carefully. Bring to boil once and remove immediately.

Serve with rice.

9
WHAT BENGALI WIDOWS
CANNOT EAT

My father died at the beginning of a particularly radiant and colourful spring. Spring in Bengal is teasing and elusive, secret yet palpable, waiting to be discovered. The crimson and scarlet of palash and shimul flowers post the season's banners on high trees. Compared to the scented flowers of the summer and monsoon—jui, bel, chameli, kamini, gandharaj, all of which are white—these scentless spring flowers are flamboyantly assertive with the one asset they have: colour. My father, who was a retiring, unassuming man, took great pleasure in their bold, flaunting reds. When I arrived in Calcutta for his funeral, I was comforted by the sight of the flowers in full bloom along the road from the airport.

That first evening back home, my mother and I sat out on our roof, talking. As darkness obscured all colours, the breeze became gusty, laden with unsettling scents from out-of-season potted flowers on neighbouring roofs. My mother had always been dynamic, forceful, efficient: the family's principal breadwinner for nearly thirty years, she had risen above personal anxiety and ignored social disapproval to allow me, alone, young and unmarried, to pursue my studies in the United States. Yet overnight she had been transformed into the archetypal Bengali widow: meek, faltering, hollow-cheeked, sunken-eyed, the woman in white from whose life all colour and pleasure must evaporate.

During the thirteen days of mourning that precede the Hindu rituals of *shraddha*, the last rites, and the subsequent *niyambhanga* (literally, the breaking of rules), all members of the bereaved family live ascetically on one main meal a day of rice and vegetables cooked together in an earthen pot with no spices except sea salt, and no oil, only a touch of ghee. The sanction against oil embraces its cosmetic use too, and for me, the roughness of my mother's parched skin and hair made her colourless appearance excruciating. But what disturbed me most was the eagerness with which she seemed to be embracing the trappings of bereavement. Under the curious, observant and critical eyes of female relatives, neighbours and visitors, she appeared to be mortifying her flesh almost joyfully, as if those thirteen days were a preparation for the future. As if it is utterly logical for a woman to lose her self and plunge into a life of ritual suffering once her husband is dead.

Hindu tradition in Bengal holds that the widow must strive for purity through deprivation. In contrast with the bride, who is dressed in red and, if family means permit, decked out in gold jewellery, the widow, regardless of her wealth and status, is drained of colour. Immediately after her husband's death, other women wash the *sindoor* (the vermilion powder signalling married status) from the parting in the widow's hair. All jewellery is removed, and she exchanges her coloured or patterned sari for the permanent, unvarying uniform of the *thaan*, borderless yards of blank white cotton. Thus transformed, she remains, for the rest of her life, the pallid symbol of misfortune, a ghostly presence in the margins of family life.

As recently as fifty years ago, widows were also forced to shave their heads as part of a socially prescribed move towards androgyny. Both of my grandfather's sisters were widowed in their twenties: my childhood memories of them are of two nearly identical creatures wrapped in shroud-like white who emerged from their village a couple of times a year and came to visit us in the city. Whenever the thaan covering their heads slipped, I would be overcome with an urge to rub my hands over their prickly scalps, resembling the spherical, yellow, white-bristled flowers of the kadam tree in our garden.

Until the Hindu Widow Remarriage Act was passed in 1856, widows were forbidden to marry for a second time. But for more than a hundred years after the act became law, it did not translate into any kind of widespread social reality (unlike the 1829 edict abolishing the burning of widows on the same pyre as their dead husbands, the infamous practice of 'suttee'). Rural Bengali households were full of widows who were no more than children, because barely pubescent girls often found themselves married to men old enough to be their fathers.

It was not until the morning before the actual shraddha ceremony that I was forced to confront the most cruel of the rules imposed on the widow by the Sanskrit *shastras*, the body of rules and rituals of Hindu life to which have been added innumerable folk beliefs. One of my aunts took me aside and asked if my mother had made up her mind to give up eating fish and meat—amish, non-vegetarian food, forbidden for widows. With a sinking heart, I realized that the image of the widow had taken such a hold of my mother that she was only too likely to embrace a vegetarian diet, all the more so because she had always loved fish and had been praised for the way she cooked it. If I said nothing, she would never again touch those wonders of the Bengali kitchen—*shorshe-ilish* (hilsa with mustard) *maachher jhol, galda chingrir malaikari* (prawns in coconut gravy), *lau-chingri* (shrimps with squash), *doi-maachh* (yogurt fish), *maachher kalia* (fish in a rich sauce). It was an unbearable thought.

The vegetarian stricture is not considered a hardship in most regions of India where the majority, particularly the Brahmins and some of the upper castes, has always been vegetarian. But Bengal is blessed with innumerable rivers crisscrossing a fertile delta, and famed for its rice and its fish. Even Brahmins have lapsed in Bengal by giving in to the regional taste for fish, which plays a central part in both the diet and the culinary imagination of the country. Fish, in its ubiquity, symbolism and variety, becomes, for the Bengali widow, the finest instrument of torture.

Several other items are forbidden to widows simply because of their associations with amish. *Puishak*, for instance, spinach-like leafy greens often cooked with small shrimps or the fried head of a hilsa fish, is disallowed. So are onion and garlic, which were eschewed by most Hindus until the last century because of their association with meat-loving Muslims, and also for their alleged lust-inducing properties, which make them totally undesirable for widows. Lentils, a good source of protein in the absence of meat, are also taboo—a stricture which might stem from the widespread practice of spicing them with chopped onion.

Social historians have speculated that these dietary restrictions served a more sinister function than simply that of moving a widow towards a state of purity: they would also lead to malnutrition, thus reducing her life span. A widow often has property, and her death would inevitably benefit *someone*—her sons, her siblings, her husband's family. And in the case of a young widow, the sooner she moves on to the next world, the less the risk of any moral transgression and ensuing scandal.

My grandmother lived the last twenty-seven of her eighty-two years as a widow, obeying every stricture imposed by rule and custom. The memory of her bleak, pinched, white-robed widowhood intensified my determination to prevent my mother from embracing a similar fate. I particularly remember a scene from my early teens when I, an only child, was living with an extended family of parents, uncles and aunts—and my grandmother. It had been a punishingly hot and dry summer. During the day, the asphalt on the streets would melt, sticking to my sandals as I walked. Night brought sweat-drenched sleeplessness and the maddening itchiness of prickly heat. Relief would come only with the eagerly awaited monsoon.

The rains came early one morning—dark, violent, lightning-streaked, fragrant and beautiful. The cook rushed to the market and came back with a big hilsa, which was cut up and fried, the crispy, flavourful pieces served at lunchtime with khichuri. This is the traditional way to celebrate the arrival of the monsoon. Though I knew my grandmother did not eat fish, I was amazed on this occasion to see that she did not touch the khichuri or the eggplant fritters or the fried potatoes. These were vegetarian items, and I had seen her eat them before on other cool, wet days. This time she ate, in her usual solitary spot, luchis that looked stale, along with some equally unappetizing cold cooked vegetables.

Why? I asked in outrage. And my mother explained that this was because of a rare coincidence: the rains had arrived on the first day of Ambubachi, the three-day period in the Bengali month of Asharh that, according to the almanac, marks the beginning of the rainy season. The ancients visualized this as the period of the earth's receptive fertility, when the summer sun vanishes, the skies open and mingle with the parched land to produce a red or brown fluid flow of earth and water, nature's manifestation of menstruating femininity. How right then for widows to suffer more than usual at such a time. They were not allowed to cook during the three-day period, and, although they were allowed to eat some foods that had been prepared in advance, boiled rice was absolutely forbidden. Since nature rarely conforms to the calculations of the almanac, I had never noticed these Ambubachi strictures being observed on the long-awaited rainy day.

The almanac was an absolute necessity for conforming to the standards of ritual purity, and my grandmother consulted it assiduously. On the day before Ambubachi started, she would prepare enough luchis and vegetables for three midday meals. Sweet yogurt and fruit, mixed with *chira*——dried, flattened rice——were also permissible. That first night of monsoon, newly aware of the sanctions of Ambubachi, I went to look for my grandmother around dinner time. All she ate was a small portion of *kheer*, milk that had been boiled down to nearly solid proportions, and some pieces of mango. I had hoped she would at least be permitted one of her favourite evening meals—— warm milk mixed with mango pulp. But no. Milk cannot be heated, for the widow's food must not receive the touch of fire during Ambubachi. The kheer, a traditional way of preserving milk, had been prepared for her the day before.

It is true that despite deprivations, household drudgery and the imposition of many fasts, widows sometimes live to a great age, and the gifted cooks among them have contributed greatly to the range, originality and subtlety of Hindu vegetarian cooking in Bengal. A nineteenth-century food writer once said that it was impossible to taste the full glory of vegetarian food unless your own wife became a widow. And Bengali literature is full of references to elderly widows whose magic touch can transform the most mundane or bitter of vegetables into nectar, and whose subtlety with spices cannot be matched.

But however glorious these concoctions, no married woman envied the widow's fate. And until recently, most widows remained imprisoned within the austere bounds of their imposed diets. Even if they were consumed with temptation or resentment, fear of discovery and public censure were enough to inhibit them.

I felt the power of public opinion as I watched my mother during the day of the shraddha. My aunt, who had been widowed when fairly young, had been bold enough, with the encouragement of her three daughters, to continue eating fish.

But I knew that my mother and many of her cronies would find it far less acceptable for a woman in her seventies not to give up *amish* in her widowhood. As one who lived abroad, in America, I also knew that my opinion was unlikely to carry much weight. But I was determined that she should not be deprived of fish, and with the support of my aunt and cousins I prepared to fight.

The crucial day of the *niyambhanga*, the third day after the *shraddha*, came. On this day, members of the bereaved family invite all their relatives to lunch, and an elaborate meal is served, representing the transition between the austerity of mourning and normal life—for everyone except the widow. Since we wanted to invite many people who were not relatives, we arranged to have two catered meals, lunch and dinner, the latter for friends and neighbours. My mother seemed to recover some of her former energy that day, supervising everything with efficiency, attending to all the guests. But she hardly touched any food. After the last guest had left, and the caterers had packed up their equipment, leaving enough food to last us for two or three days, I asked her to sit down and eat dinner with me. For the first time since my father's death, the two of us were absolutely alone in the house. I told her I would serve the food; I would be the grown-up now.

She smiled and sat down at the table. I helped her to rice and dal, then to two of the vegetable dishes. She held up her hand then. No more. I was not to go on to the fish. Silently, we ate. She asked for a little more rice and vegetables. I complied, then lifted a piece of rui fish and held it over her plate. Utter panic filled her eyes, and she shot anxious glances around the room. She told me, vehemently, to eat the fish myself.

It was that panic-stricken look around her own house, where she was alone with me, her daughter, that filled me with rage.

I was determined to vanquish the oppressive force of ancient belief, reinforced by whatever model of virtue she had inherited from my grandmother. We argued for what seemed like hours, my voice rising, she asking me to be quiet for fear of the neighbours, until finally I declared that I would never touch any amish myself as long as she refused to eat fish. The mother who could not bear the thought of her child's deprivation eventually prevailed, though the woman still quaked with fear of sin and retribution.

I have won a small victory, but I have lost the bigger battle. My mother's enjoyment of food, particularly of fish, as well as her joyful exuberance in the kitchen where her labours produced such memorable creations, have vanished. Sometimes, as I sit and look at her, I see a procession of silent women in white going back through the centuries. They live as household drudges, slaves in the kitchen and the field; they are ostracized even in their own homes during weddings or other happy ceremonies, their very presence considered an invitation to misfortune. In the dim corners they inhabit, they try to contain their hunger. Several times a year, they fast and pray and prepare feasts for priests and Brahmins, all in the hope of escaping widowhood in the next life. On the eleventh day of each moon, they deny themselves food and water and shed tears over their unhappy fate, while women with husbands make a joyous ritual out of eating rice and fish. Their anguish and anger secreted in the resinous chamber of fear, these white-clad women make their gradual journey towards death.

10
HOW BENGAL DISCOVERED
CHHANA

Ask any Indian and you will be told that Bengal excels in the taste and variety of its milk-based sweets. Of these, the sweets made from chhana (cottage cheese or acid-curd cheese) are unique to the region. Nowhere else in India does the confectioner work such magic through manipulating this substance which is derived by cutting milk with acid. And since vegetarians as well as fish- and meat-eaters relish sweets, Bengal's chhana-based concoctions have long been famed outside the region. Two sweets, in particular, *sandesh* and *rosogolla*, are practically synonymous with the sweet-toothed Bengali, with his longstanding reputation as an indolent, easygoing, comfort-loving gourmet.

But what is the reason for the pre-eminence of chhana in this eastern corner of the Indian subcontinent? And why is it not associated with sweet-making in the rest of the country? The answer lies in an encounter between two races—historic, yet forgotten by most Bengalis today. It began five hundred years ago, when the Portuguese explorer, Vasco da Gama, landed on the western coast of India in 1498. To fully realize its significance, we need to understand the long-held beliefs about the nature of milk that prevailed among the people of this region.

Just as in medieval European physiology, the four humours—blood, phlegm, choler, and bile—were thought to be the constituents of the human body, their respective proportions determining an individual's character, mood, and health, similarly, in the ancient Indian system of Ayurveda, the body is dominated by one of three elements—*sattva*, *raujas*, and *taumas*—each imparting specific characteristics. And extending the notion that we are what we eat, the ancients ascribed those same characteristics to different foods. In this hierarchical universe, milk (including its derivatives, ghee, buttermilk, cream, yogurt) is easily in the top bracket. It is the purest of edibles whose quality is *sattvika* (descriptive form of sattva): nutritive, agreeable, conducive to serenity and spirituality. Sages and ascetics, who left all worldly ties behind and isolated themselves in the wilderness in search of higher metaphysical truths, subsisted on milk provided by local devotees. Milk was the one food that would not induce worldly desires or distractions in their minds. This belief in the semi-sacred quality of milk is also reflected in its consistent use as an offering to the gods. Rice pudding, for instance, is one of the commonest items offered to important household deities like Lakshmi, the goddess of wealth and prosperity. Even outside of Hinduism, milk retains its connotation of purity. The first food with which the Buddha broke his long fast after achieving Nirvana was milk-based.

A famous turn-of-the century Bengali food writer, Bipradas Mukhopadhyay, in his 1906 book, *Mishtanno Pak* (Making Sweets), documents the different types of milk and their specific qualities as set down by the ancients. Starting with the milk of cows, goats, and ewes, the list goes on to enumerate water buffaloes, camels, mares, female elephants and women as acceptable sources of milk for human consumption. Cow's milk, as one would expect, is defined as second only to human milk in its wide-ranging benefits. Whatever the source, all milk was believed to have several properties in common: tasty, soothing, energizing, cool, rich, sperm-generating, reducing bile and gout, and conducive to phlegm.

Milk was also an important part of the diet of ordinary people. Unlike the ascetic, the householder looked on milk with infinite desire. It was not only health food par excellence, it had powerful symbolic value as an image of achievable prosperity. In agriculture-based Bengal, 'milk-and-rice' became synonymous with the sustenance of a comfortable life. Vegetarians and non-vegetarians alike considered milk a precious food. Both the folktales as well as the substantial body of orally transmitted ditties (*chharas*) of Bengal are replete with images of milk that connote plenty and prosperity. Kings are anointed with milk and butter before their coronation. Princesses bathe in copiously flowing milk. Young girls hope to improve their complexion by washing their faces with milk. Mothers who suddenly encounter lost children after many years find their breasts spouting milk. Rivers of milk, rippling waves of milk, lakes of milk, trembling layers of thickened milk, even oceans of milk recur with amazing frequency in myths, folktales, poems, and songs.

A famous Bengali folktale, recounting the adventures of two young princes named Sheet and Basanta (also the words for Winter and Spring, respectively), demonstrates the extraordinarily vivid presence of milk in the folk imagination. Separated from his older brother Sheet, Basanta was discovered in the woods by a holy man who raised him as his disciple. One day, sitting under a tree, Basanta heard two parrots talking to each other about a fabulous gem that the king of the elephants carried on his head. Anyone who got hold of it would be able to marry the beautiful princess Rupabati. Immediately, Basanta decided to set off in search of this gem. After travelling for twelve years and thirteen days, he reached the realm of the royal elephant. But a huge, white mountain barred the way. Down its body flowed cascades of milk; its peak was smothered in quivering layers of *sar* (the thick skin skimmed off from the top as heated milk cools down). Basanta climbed to the top and saw on the other side an expansive ocean filled with thick, rich milk. In that ocean bloomed thousands of fragrant golden lotuses and in their midst frolicked a beautiful, milk-white elephant, on whose head glowed a gem that seemed brighter than all the jewels of the world put together. But as soon as Basanta jumped into the ocean of milk, it became a sandy desert.

An ancient tale from the Mahabharata describes how the gods and demons got together to churn the ocean of milk in the hope of obtaining ambrosia which would make them immortal. But after hauling up many wondrous treasures—including the sacred pitcher of ambrosia—a virulent poison, distilled from the venom of all the serpents who ruled the underworld, rose to the surface. And immediately, the ocean of milk was transformed into the expanse of salt water that we mortals know today.

Both these stories illustrate a deep conviction about the fragility of milk. The introduction of an alien element destroys the very nature of the life-giving, life-sustaining fluid. Deliberately doing so, could, therefore, easily be deemed sacrilegious. For many centuries, the importance of that belief was instrumental in limiting the people of Bengal (as well as of the rest of India) in the uses they found for milk and the products they derived from it.

The use of milk and the general beliefs about its properties continued unchanged into the medieval period, as can be seen from literary evidence. Medieval Bengali literature abounds in long narrative poems. Some of them are full of descriptions of food that highlight the connection between human temperament and the nature of food and here, too, milk and its derivatives—ghee, yoghurt, or buttermilk—exemplify the nobler qualities. In the sixteenth-century *Chandimangalkabya*, written by Mukundaram Chakrabarti, descriptions of meals include those prepared for Shiva and Vishnu. Shiva, who is considered choleric and prone to violence, eats food cooked with pungent mustard oil, not ghee. Vishnu, on the other hand, is imagined as having a serene temperament and is offered sattvika foods including tender vegetables cooked in ghee, and a variety of desserts, all derived from milk.

These medieval poems refer to many desserts that followed elaborate meals, and milk was the basis for quite a few. Rice pudding—called *paramanno*, meaning the ultimate rice or best rice, in both Sanskrit and Bengali—was not only offered to the gods but was also a human favourite. It was a feature of most festive meals and many secular rituals. So was sweetened yogurt, which (along with its unsweetened version) had highly auspicious connotations. But the commonest material for making sweets was kheer, that is, milk which has been boiled down and reduced until it is either a thick, viscous liquid (similar to what is sold as evaporated milk in western supermarkets), or a tight, slightly grainy solid. This latter version is often called *khoa kheer* and has the virtue of remaining unspoiled much longer than any other form of milk, an important consideration in a humid, tropical climate.

The evidence is bolstered by another famous medieval work of literature, neither mythic nor fictional, but a biography in narrative verse. The *Chaitanyacharitamrita* by Krishnadas Kabiraj recounts the life and times of the remarkable religious reformer known as Sri Chaitanya. Born into an orthodox Hindu brahman family of Vedic scholars, Chaitanya rejected the strict hierarchy and cruel discrimination of the Hindu caste system. He preached a message of equality, brotherhood, love, and non-violence. The oppressed members of the lower castes followed him in droves and emulated his personal habits, which included strict vegetarianism, a practice not common until then—even among brahmans—in fish-loving Bengal.

The importance of this biography to historians of Bengali food is immeasurable. When barely out of his teens, Krishnadas Kabiraj became a devout follower of Chaitanya. The latter took him everywhere he went, including the homes of other wealthy disciples. This provided Krishnadas with an intimate knowledge of every aspect of Chaitanya's daily life. In the biography, he describes in fascinating detail the numerous elaborate vegetarian meals prepared for Chaitanya in the homes of admirers. A staggering variety of sweets are mentioned, indicating that despite his abjuration of human intimacy and worldly possessions, Chaitanya had a Bengali predilection for sweets. Many of these were made with puffed, popped, or flaked rice, combined with white or brown sugar and/or kheer. Others were concocted from flour, coconut, ground legumes, or sesame seeds. Krishnadas also mentions an impressive array of purely milk-based sweets—kheer mixed with sliced mangos, sweet yogurt, and items like *dugdha-laklaki*, *sarbhaja*, *sarpupee*, and *sandesh*.

For those unfamiliar with Bengali food, some explanation of these terms is required in order to appreciate the point made earlier, the taboo on making a deliberate, invasive change to the nature of milk which, clearly, still prevailed at this time. Three of the sweets served to Chaitanya—*dugdha-laklaki* (known today as *raabri*), *sarbhaja*, and *sarpupee* (known today as *sarpuria*)—are mutations of sar, which is as precious to the people of the Indian subcontinent as cream is to the west. In a tropical region, before the advent of refrigeration, the only way to preserve milk (without making it into kheer) was to repeatedly boil it, the notion of pasteurization being still far into the future. A by-product of all this boiling was the transformation of the fatty top layer into a 'skin'. Each time the milk came to a boil, a new skin would form and it would be skimmed off, added to the previous layers and pressed together. These thick layers were used to make sar-based sweets. Dugdha-laklaki is layers of sar cut into squares and floating in mildly sweetened milk, sometimes flavoured with saffron. Sar fried in ghee and soaked in syrup becomes sarbhaja. Fried in ghee, layered with crushed almonds, khoa kheer, and cardamom, and then soaked in sweetened milk, it becomes sarpuria. As for the sandesh mentioned by Krishnadas Kabiraj and other contemporary writers, it was sweetened pellets of khoa kheer.

What is notable in all these descriptions is that not a single sweet is made from chhana. Modern food historians like K.T. Achaya have discussed the Aryan taboo on cutting milk with acid. It is notable that in all the myths about the young Krishna, who was brought up by foster parents among the milkmen of Brindaban (in the state of Uttar Pradesh), there are thousands of references to milk, butter, ghee, and yoghurt, but none to chhana. Even now, the practice of adding acid to make cheese is not to be seen in northern India. Sweets offered in the temples of modern Brindaban (sacred to Krishna worshippers) are invariably made of solidified kheer. In making sweets from milk, Chaitanya's medieval contemporaries were, therefore, adhering to the tradition prevalent throughout the Indian subcontinent at that point in time.

And yet, as noted earlier, whenever Bengali sweets are mentioned today, it is the chhana-based confections that everyone thinks of. The introduction of chhana into the Bengali—indeed, Indian—food universe in the centuries following Chaitanya, and its enthusiastic adoption, remains a wonderful metaphor for the enrichment of societies through encounters with the unknown.

Enter the Portuguese.

From Portugal to Bengal is a distance not only of several thousand miles, but also of climate, topography, and terrain. The connection between the two is neither obvious nor memorable. Britain, not Portugal, France, or Holland, became the dominant colonial power in India, once the East India Company had cemented its hold over Bengal following a decisive victory in the 1757 Battle of Plassey. Traders and fortune-hunters from these other European countries, however, had been coming to India long before the establishment of British control. Some formed small settlements that bear their imprint to this day— the Portuguese enclave of Goa on the western coast of India and the French enclaves of Chandannagar and Pondicherry on the east. But it was a Portuguese settlement in Bengal, so hazy in the regional memory, which made a revolutionary contribution to the region's food universe, as can be seen from trawling the byways of the past.

Although Portugal does not head the list of European countries in terms of gourmet cheeses, it does have several unique varieties. In the introduction to her book, *The Food of Spain and Portugal*, Elisabeth Lambert Ortiz talks about their excellence. Most are made of sheep or goat's milk, but cow's milk is also used. She describes the innumerable fresh cheeses, *queijos frescos*, made into little cakes about three inches in diameter. When mature, they are firm, with a strong flavour. When fresh, they are soft and spreadable. The importance of queijos frescos in the Portuguese diet is demonstrated by the migration of the product. This cheese can be found in the refrigerated food section of many speciality shops in American cities with large Portuguese communities.

Shift the scene to modern Bengal. One of the curiosities available in Calcutta's New Market (Hogg Market in the early days of British colonialism) is 'bandel cheese'. It comes in the form of little cakes of fresh cow's milk cheese, remarkably similar to the kind mentioned by Elisabeth Lambert Ortiz. But ask the shopkeepers why the cheese is called 'bandel' or what its origins are, and they are likely to be stumped. Certainly most people buying the cheese are not aware of any possible connection between this product and the Portuguese traders who followed Vasco da Gama and settled in large numbers in Bengal during the sixteenth and seventeenth centuries. Nor does the average consumer realize that the numerous sweets made from chhana that s/he loves are, in a sense, the siblings or cousins of this same 'bandel cheese.'

But each time the Bengali rolls his or her tongue around the spongy juiciness of a rosogolla, or revels in the delicate graininess of a sandesh, the forgotten encounter between two races comes to life. For the Portuguese not only contributed the comparatively obscure 'bandel cheese' to the gourmet Bengali's platter, their distinctive way of processing milk also initiated a whole new flowering of the Bengali culinary imagination.

The advent of European traders permanently changed many aspects of eating in the Indian subcontinent. Not only was it a case of East meeting West in terms of diet and cookery, it also meant a significant enlargement of the subcontinent's food repertoire. For the Europeans, who came in search of eastern spices, brought with them the vegetables they had discovered in the New World. The earliest and foremost traders were, of course, the Portuguese who discovered the direct sea route from Europe to Asia. For almost the entire sixteenth century, Portugal virtually monopolized this route.

During that time, they spread their area of operations along both coasts of India. In the east, they settled in large numbers in Bengal, along the Hooghly river. Initially, they had a fearsome reputation in Bengal, since some of them used their navigational skills to commit daring acts of piracy along the coast as well as in the interior where the numerous rivers served as primary conduits for goods and passengers. Many of the Portuguese also intermarried with the locals, thus paving the way for a more intimate exchange between the two races. Among the new crops they introduced were tobacco, potato, cashew, papaya, guava, and a host of vegetables.

Modern compendiums on the cheeses of the world stress the paucity of cheeses in the cuisine of Asia, a fact attributed to the humid tropical climate, which made it difficult to apply the sophisticated preservation techniques needed for the famous cheeses of Europe. Among the few cheeses found in the Indian subcontinent today are the ubiquitous *paneer* (familiar to westerners through the good offices of Indian restaurants serving dishes like *mattar-paneer* and *saag-paneer*), a couple of varieties from Gujarat, and two from Bengal.

Books like the Simon and Schuster *Pocket Guide to Cheese* and Geoffrey Campbell-Platt's *Fermented Foods of the World* refer to the two cheeses of Bengal as chhana and *bandal*. Both are described as 'acid-curd cheeses' made from cow or buffalo milk, although no mention is made of how they came into being.

Bandal, however, is pronounced *bandel* in Bengali and a little digging reveals that it is cheese that is made only in Bandel, a town situated twenty-five miles north of Calcutta on the banks of the Hooghly. The name derives from the Bengali term bandar, meaning port. The Portuguese had originally chosen the nearby town of Hooghly (which they called Ugolim) as their centre of operations. But in 1632 they suffered a serious defeat at the hands of the imperial Mughal army. They then retreated to Bandel, which was, at the time, the chief port on the Hooghly, and formed a second, more lasting establishment. The reason for Bandel's continued popularity as a settlement, among not only the Portuguese but also other Europeans, was its supposed salubrious qualities. Many of them went there to convalesce and recover from the trying effects of the local climate. A report in the *Calcutta Gazette* of 3 September 1799, for example, says, 'Sir Robert Chambers, Judge of the Supreme Court, had gone to spend the vacation at the pleasant and healthy settlement of Bandel.'

Today, the chief relic of this flourishing Portuguese colony is the Bandel Church, the oldest Christian church in Bengal. The present structure, according to some historians, replaced an older one built by the Portuguese in their fort in 1599, which was razed to the ground by the Mughal army on the capture of the town in 1632. The present church and monastery are said to have been built in 1660 by Gomez de Soto, who had managed to save the keystone of the old church, bearing the date 1599, during the sack of the town.

K. T. Achaya documents the establishment of the Portuguese community in Bengal: 'By the second half of the seventeenth century, they [the Portuguese settlers] numbered 20,000' with some at Rajmahal. 'They loved cottage cheese, which they made by "breaking" milk with acidic materials. This routine technique may have lifted the Aryan taboo on deliberate milk curdling and given the traditional Bengali *moira* [confectioner] a new raw material to work with.'

Given this well-established presence, the influence of Portuguese cooking techniques on the eating habits of Bengal is not surprising. It was noted by at least one contemporary travel writer. Francois Bernier, a French doctor, spent seven years in India from 1659 to 1666. He mentions in detail the physical beauty of Bengal and its lush plenitude of grains, vegetables, fish, and meat. He also notes: 'Bengal likewise is celebrated for its sweetmeats, especially in places inhabited by the Portuguese, who are skilful in the art of preparing them and with whom they are an article of considerable trade.'

Although bandal (or bandel) cheese is now associated with West Bengal (and found only in a few speciality shops), the process of making acid-curd cheeses found another incarnation across the border in the eastern part of Bengal—the famous Dhakai paneer. Dhaka, the capital of modern Bangladesh, was known as Rajmahal during the sixteenth and seventeenth centuries when the Portuguese began settling in Bengal. Dhakai paneer, as described in the Simon and Schuster *Pocket Guide to Cheese*, is made from cow or buffalo milk, or a mixture of the two. It is drained in wicker or bamboo baskets, pressed, and dried for about two weeks, before being smoked. Wedges of salt, placed in the middle, help preserve it and lend sharpness to the taste. The cheese is eaten plain, or sliced and fried gently in clarified butter, or even added to legume and vegetable dishes. Both Dhakai paneer and bandel cheese, however, remain speciality products and not common items for regular consumption in any part of Bengal.

Neither, however, can be made without curdling milk with acid. It is the solid separated by curdling, that the Bengalis called chhana, which has found such wide application in Bengali sweet production and left an entire region indebted to the Portuguese. The etymology of the term is rather obscure, but according to several major Bengali dictionaries, it is a case of a verb becoming a noun. Chhana is related to another verb, *shana*. Both mean kneading vigorously by hand to create a fine paste or dough. The naming of chhana seems based on the fact that all chhana-based sweets require the curdled milk solid to be first kneaded. In fact, the excellence of many sweets depends on the right degree of kneading and often the reputation or status of a Bengali moira depended on his success in achieving the right consistency of kneaded chhana respective to the sweet being made from it. It is also of interest that the word chhana has a separate meaning in colloquial Bengali—children or offspring. And if one considers curdled milk to be the 'offspring' of untreated milk, then this is indeed a serendipitous example of double entendre.

In one of the stories of *The Book of Thousand Nights and One Night*, a beautiful female slave called Sympathy the Learned is brought to the court of the Khalifa Harun-al-Rashid and quizzed by a series of scholars and wise men on different branches of knowledge. In answering the questions of a doctor about the treatment and prevention of disease, Sympathy says that gluttony is the cause of all disease. To avoid gluttony, one has to divide the belly into three parts, one to be filled with food, one with water, and one with nothing at all so that the body has room to breathe and the soul can lodge comfortably.

Whatever one may think of the efficacy of this charming formulation (which is not so far from modern directives of health), the image of the Bengali moira is that of a man at the other end of the spectrum. A mountainous figure with a ballooning middle, he gives the impression that all three parts of his belly are more than full. He is a famously sedentary character, sitting all day in front of his stove, surrounded by huge containers filled with chhana and kheer from which he concocts the infinite variety of sweets that are synonymous with gourmet eating in Bengal. Clad only in the traditional white *dhoti* from the waist down, he leaves his torso bare except for a red and white checked *gaamchha* (napkin) flung over one shoulder and used frequently to mop his sweating face and neck. The aphorism about the moira never eating sandesh is supposed to indicate a gluttony that has resulted in absolute satiety.

It should be noted that the sandesh today is a totally different creation from the one offered to Chaitanya and his medieval contemporaries. The latter, as mentioned above, was made from sweetened, solidified kheer. Since the dryness of the kheer made it easy to preserve, Bengalis developed the custom of carrying some sandesh with them whenever they visited someone. The term sandesh also meant news, and the sweet, therefore, became the perfect offering for a visitor bearing news, or interested in getting the host's news.

Chhana has different consistencies. As Achaya notes, 'mild precipitation of milk using whey yields a soft but perishable chhana product, while the use of lime juice yields a gritty one which sets to a hard, long-lasting product.' It is hard to determine exactly when the term sandesh came to indicate a sweet made with chhana rather than with kheer. But it is reasonable to assume that it had become common usage by the latter half of the nineteenth century. Today, the simplest Bengali sandesh is the *kanchagolla* (literally, 'uncooked ball'), that is, hot, sweetened chhana formed into round balls. The term *kancha* (uncooked) does not indicate a lack of processing by heat after the milk has been curdled. The chhana is actually tossed lightly with sugar over low heat and the mastery of a moira is indicated by the complexity of texture he can achieve despite the shortness of the cooking/processing time. Some of the best kanchagolla is available from sweet shops around the famous Kali temple in Calcutta's Kalighat neighbourhood. They are generally given as offerings to the goddess. Once they have gone through the ritual of offering, the devotees are free to eat and enjoy these soft yet grainy rounded shapes served on disposable plates of shaal leaves, their milky flavour curiously enhanced by the slightly smoky odour of the leaf container.

In more elaborate incarnations, the chhana for sandesh can be pressed, dried, flavoured with fruit essences, coloured, cooked to many different consistencies, filled with syrup, blended with coconut or kheer, and moulded into a variety of shapes (including those of elephants, conch shells, and tigers). Fancy confectioners in Calcutta or Dhaka even take proprietary pride in a particular shape or flavour of sandesh as their particular invention. The Bengali obsession with this sweet is indicated in the flights of fancy displayed in the naming of different kinds of sandesh. Bipradas Mukhopadhyay, writing in 1906, lists more than twenty names, based on the form, content, consistency, and flavour of the sandesh. Among the most memorable are: *abaar khabo* (I want to eat it again), *pranohara* (robber of my soul), *manoranjan* (heart's delight), *nayantara* (pupil of my eye), and *ahladey putul* (pampered doll). In the heydays of colonial rule, the British, too, were honoured, as indicated by names such as 'good morning' and 'Lord Ripon.'

Chhana-based sweets in Bengal (including both West Bengal and Bangladesh) are too numerous to enumerate in full. But some of the most famous deserve mention. Next to sandesh, the rosogolla is the best known as the representative sweet from Bengal. Its most obvious characteristic is that of being soaked in syrup (*ros*). The other is the exquisite smoothness of the chhana. There is no room for graininess in a good rosogolla. A variety referred to as the sponge rosogolla (*sic*) is considered the best. Other syrup-soaked sweets made from chhana include *chamcham, pantua, chhanabora, chhanar jilipi, rosomundi, golapjaam*, and *kalojaam*. Sometimes the fame of a sweet is tied to the name of a place, as in the '*kanchagolla* of Natore,' the '*monda* of Muktagachha', the '*chamcham* of Tangail.' Sometimes it is the name of a shop that serves as a label of excellence, as in the sandesh from Bhim Chandra Nag or the rosogolla from K. C. Das.

One interesting point of speculation is why these sweets are rarely made at home, for the true subtlety and excellence of most Bengali foods (vegetables, legumes, fish, meat, and sweets not made from chhana) is generally to be found in home cooking. According to the eminent Bangladeshi historian, the late Professor Abdur Razzaque, it was the professional sweetmakers—many of them Muslims—rather than the home cook, who were originally responsible for the creation of all these chhana-based sweets. This seems likely when one considers that Hindu households, with all their practices of ritual purity, might initially have resisted the invasion of the kitchen by a substance made by the Portuguese 'heathens.' It would thus be left to the professionals, working in a shop and not a home, to experiment with a new medium of gustatory delight. The practice, once started, still prevails. And capitalizing on the enduring Bengali addiction for the varied, delightful offspring of chhana, sweet shops flourish in every corner of a city or town in West Bengal and Bangladesh. The home cook need only step out to buy any chhana-based sweets he fancies and, therefore, has little incentive to invest time, energy, and skill in making them.

The arrival of Vasco da Gama in India signalled many pivotal developments in the history of Europe and Asia, including the sad scourge of colonialism. But today, in the combined glow of a post-millennial and pre-millennial light of enquiry, the Bengalis, at least, can savour a very special sweetness that is the gift of the Portuguese.

SANDESH

INGREDIENTS

4½ litres of milk
340 grams of sugar
2 or three limes, cut into wedges

METHOD

To make chhana for sandesh, heat the milk in a heavy-bottomed pan. When it comes to boil, stir with a spatula and start squeezing the juice of the limes into it. Keep stirring, so that the milk does not boil over from the pan.

When the milk separates into liquid whey and solid chhana, remove the pan and pour the contents into a colander. When it is cool enough to handle, remove the chhana, tie it up in a cheesecloth, and press as much of the excess water out as possible. Let the bundle hang for half an hour to get rid of all the moisture.

Take out the chhana, put it in a mixing bowl and knead it with your hands until it is a fine paste. Judging how fine the paste should be is an art that comes only with practice. Heat a wok over medium low heat, add the kneaded chhana and the sugar, and fry, stirring constantly. When the mixture comes away easily from the sides of the wok and the sugar has been absorbed completely, remove from the stove. Before removing, you may add some rose water or Indian kewra water to flavour the sandesh. Pour the mixture onto a plate and while still warm, divide into equal portions and form balls. In Bengal, special wooden or clay moulds are used to give a variety of shapes to sandesh.

11

FOOD, RITUAL AND ART IN BENGAL

Parallel aesthetic visions are called up by the conjunction of food and art. There are direct depictions of food in art, in painting, literature, cinema. Conversely, there is the artistry of preparing and presenting food. But all such convergence of food and art, however sublime, is about food as an object of consumption and sustenance, either in the immediate present, or savoured as a memory, or anticipated as a future pleasure. But there is a third dimension, where food is the medium for depicting the emotional, ceremonial, and ritual universe of a people. It is a realm where, having already experienced the pleasures of preparing, presenting, and partaking, one has subsequently made it into a versatile medium for both spiritual and artistic creativity, a metaphor for diverse human experiences. As in the simple and complex conjunctions of food and art among the Hindus of Bengal.

The traditional life of Bengal is rich in form, ritual, and aestheticism. In sacred and secular ceremonies, Bengalis have invested food with intricate symbolic significance. An extraordinarily active folk imagination draws on food images to create verse, paintings, and craft objects.

Gurusaday Dutt, a member of the Indian Civil Service in pre-independence India, wrote about his own discoveries of the entwining of art, ritual, and ceremony in rural Bengal in the course of his official travels throughout the region between 1929 and 1933. He made a careful study of the artistic and musical traditions of the villages he visited—traditions that the Western-educated urban elite of that time was barely aware of and certainly did not value. And he made it his mission to preserve these traditions, support their practitioners, and focus public attention on them. In the course of his observations, he realized that in this pre-eminently rural region of the Indian subcontinent, almost every aspect of life, however mundane, was an aesthetic ritual. Food, in that cultural mindset, was not only something to be consumed for survival, but also an artistic medium. It provided the raw material for painting and making offerings to the gods; it enhanced personal experience when its shape, colour, and life became metaphors for human existence; it acquired symbolic meaning and enriched social customs with ceremonial value. And the creative force that was behind such transformations was a rurally derived folk imagination, not the cultivated, educated, sophisticated mindset of intellectuals.

'The most outstanding feature of the art of rural Bengal,' wrote Gurusaday Dutt, 'consists in its being synonymous with the life of the people—their beliefs and their religion, their daily activities and their seasonal and social festivities, their work and their play. The whole of life was conceived as an art and lived as an art.'

For many years after he recorded his observations, things did not change very much. Young girls in rural areas, as well as in the more traditional urban families, were painstakingly trained in the art of domestic ritual and ceremony, many of which were based on an innate respect for food—particularly the staple, rice, which had immense symbolic significance. An agrarian social structure that remained largely unchanged over the centuries, despite the larger events of history sweeping over the Indian subcontinent, created a continuous collective consciousness that is to be seen in indigenous artistic endeavours, such as the making of quilts, the decoration of homesteads, the composition of verses, the devising of innumerable rituals around the major events of life (weddings, births, and deaths), and the worship of the gods. Food, whether in its raw form or modified through human preparation, runs as a constant motif through these modes of artistic expression.

A common Bengali adage refers to thirteen festivals in

twelve months. Thirteen, of course, is an apocryphal number. Festive rituals abound throughout the year and vary not only from village to village, but sometimes even from family to family. The festivals range from the strictly religious (the worship of specific deities in the Hindu pantheon), to the semi-sacred (the observance, usually by women, of certain auspicious days in the lunar calendar, or the practice of rituals in connection with a *brata* or undertaking/vow), to the entirely secular (weddings, birthdays, an infant's first meal of rice, etc.). On all these occasions, village homes, whether rich or poor, are decorated with intricate patterns rich in symbolism and artfulness. Traditionally, this is done by women and highlights an imagination based on an acute observation and appreciation of the natural world and its products.

Almost every visible area of the cottage—the patio, the wooden columns supporting the roof, the floor of rooms where guests and relatives will assemble, walls, and alcoves, as well as objects like wooden seats and large pitchers of water, are decorated with patterns in a style known as *alpana* (derived from the Sanskrit *alimpana*, ornamental plastering). And the artistic medium for such patterns is the staple food of Bengal, rice. Only *atap* (non-parboiled) rice is used, usually of the short-grained variety. The rice is soaked in water to soften, then dried, and ground to a fine powder which is held between the thumb and the tip of the index finger and sprinkled on the ground to create the patterns the artist has in mind. Reminiscent of the religio-artistic practices of Tibetan monks, this technique is called *gunrichitra* or *dhulichitra* (particle painting or dust painting) in Bengal. A more durable medium is created when the rice powder is mixed with water to make a thick paste. A rag, folded to form a tapering wick, is held in the hollow of the palm, its pointed end being dipped into the rice paste and used to paint the alpana patterns. Once dried, the patterns show up vividly white on earthen floors, wooden surfaces, or terracotta objects. Occasionally, coloured dyes are added to the white rice paste.

The drawing of alpanas is always spontaneous. They represent a continuous tradition of artistic form and technique among the women of Bengal and the spontaneity of drawing is a crucial aspect of the art. There is no template to refer to, nor any previously documented pattern to copy—only the knowledge of patterns seen in the past and a community memory of motifs developed through the ages. Among the common motifs are the flowers, leaves, fruits, and vegetables that are a part of the landscape. Ears of rice, as is only to be expected, show up often, as do rice storage containers (*dhaner morai*) as symbols of plenty. For the artist, the act of decorating a space or an object for a ceremonial purpose is vested with as much ritual significance as the eventual ceremony itself. And the choice of rice (paste) as the primary medium of painting reaffirms the importance of this crop in Bengal's life, a significance that has led to rice being considered synonymous with Lakshmi, the goddess of wealth, prosperity, and grace. Even when sated, Bengalis are reluctant to waste or discard the portion of rice on their plates, lest the goddess perceive it as an insult and withdraw her favours.

Another remarkable example of the union of food and folk imagination in art can be seen in the rich and varied collection of chharas, songs and rhymes that are part of a long-lived oral tradition in Bengal. Only in the late nineteenth and early twentieth centuries were these rhymes collected and documented in a systematic fashion. Foremost among the rescuers of chharas were the poet Rabindranath Tagore and his nephew, Abanindranath Tagore. As is only to be expected, the chharas, even at their most fanciful or nonsensical, conjure up a faithful picture of an agrarian society where life was ritualized, expectations well-defined, the roles of men, women, and children unquestioned, and economic status often indicated by the food eaten every day.

The rhymes are replete with images of food, and key items recur in many forms. The region's diet includes rice, fish, vegetables, and milk and milk products. As a tropical land of many rivers, blessed with fertile alluvial soil, Bengal produced all these foods in abundance, but social and economic inequalities determined the proportion of individual access. In rhyme after rhyme, food is used to depict topography and climate, the interactions between family members (one's own as well as the dreaded in-laws), prosperity or want, and indoor and outdoor activities. It is not hard to imagine that women, who were in charge of the kitchen, were also the creators of these simple rhyming verses that so reflect their own concerns.

Fish and fishing are frequent themes. Many rhymes mention the son of the family (far more important than the daughter, who would, after all, merely get married and go away to her husband's house) setting off on a fishing expedition. And numerous verses have the same recurrent image of two large fish (rui and catla, both of the carp family) leaping out of the river. The arcing motion of these graceful, silver-scaled, piscine forms struck generations of Bengalis as one of the most beautiful sights in their riverine land. In one verse, the mother ponders what nourishing food to give her son before he sets out on a journey and decides it will be prawns caught from the river, cooked with the eggplant she has grown in her garden. A charming image of the close relationship between human beings and their environment occurs in another chhara. A young boy, trying to catch a powerful boal fish (a freshwater shark), comes to grief when the fish capsizes the boat. Disappointed, the boy comes back to the shore. This amuses an otter so much that it gleefully cavorts in the river. The boy's doting mother tells the otter to stop its antics for a moment and look towards the bank where her son, unperturbed by the loss of his boat, is dancing no less expertly. Another gem of a couplet, with an acute economy of words, evokes the image of one's dream girl whose waist is slim and supple as a pankal fish (swamp eel, a common food fish in rural Bengal).

Rice, the basis of almost all meals in Bengal, takes many forms. In addition to the variety and quality of rice types— according to some agricultural experts, the terrain is varied enough to grow 10,000 indigenous varieties of rice—the ways of processing rice help create a whole eating universe out of this one particular grain: puffed rice, rice flakes, popped rice (plain or coated with sugar), each with variants, depending on the strain of rice they are derived from and the way they are prepared and eaten. Rice flakes feature prominently in both the chharas and the folktales of Bengal because they are easy to carry for the intrepid hero setting out on his travels and because of their versatility in complementing many other foods. In the heat of a tropical summer afternoon, the flakes, soaked in cool water and accompanied by milk or yogurt, ground coconut, summer fruits like banana or mango, made a meal that was both soothing and filling. Numerous verses mention such preparations made for the visiting son-in-law (the mortal deity who held the happiness or misery of the daughter in his hands) by his attentive mother-in-law. For the traveller, rice flakes could simply be soaked in the water from a river or lake and eaten with a bit of sugar. The longer the grains and the more delicate the variety of rice, the lighter and tastier the rice flakes. In a society where the daughter-in-law was commonly victimized by her mother-in-law, many verses mention placating the latter with an array of gifts, one of them being the finest quality of flaked rice. Alas, equally numerous references to the unmitigated suffering and drudgery endured by the young bride at the hands of her mother-in-law clearly demonstrate how ineffective such gifts often were.

The cook's pride in her own art, especially in the art of preparing vegetables that the Hindu culinary tradition in Bengal is famed for, is also demonstrated in some delightful rhymes. In one verse, the speaker mentions a lightly seasoned vegetable stew of baby pumpkins or gourds—vegetables that were considered the appropriate 'cool foods' during the summer. In another, a rich merchant's daughter boasts of her special recipe for a combination dish including eggplant, green bananas, striped gourd, and climbing gourd. Beyond the normal pride of a good cook, this verse also illustrates the self-confidence, bordering on arrogance, of a woman from a wealthy family. One well-known verse is about an expert cook decrying the lack of skill of a young girl called Rani, who commits the heresies of adding hot chilli peppers to shukto, a mildly bitter dish, and ghee to ambol (a tart sauce, often tamarind-based, and always made with pungent mustard oil). It is likely that the unfortunate Rani is being castigated by one of her in-laws, who could make life miserable for a new bride with barbed comments about her lack of skills in the kitchen.

Sometimes, the cook-artist's perception of the lush vegetative world she inhabits expresses itself in innovative metaphors. Water lilies blooming in the still waters of a pond are compared to writing inscribed on paper; buds positioned around green lily pads are thought to resemble a dish of cooked greens garnished with boris—pellets of sun-dried legume paste. Spare, haiku-like verses evoke specific emotions simply by positioning discrete images, including those of food items, next to each other. In one such verse, a sister's longing for her absent brother is expressed through the contrast of torrential rain under an ominously black sky on the far side of a river, and a pepper plant loaded with vivid scarlet chilli peppers on the bank where she sits alone.

Perhaps the most repetitive food image in these chharas is that of milk and its many derivatives—yoghurt, curds, whey, clotted cream, sar, and ghee. Milk is an expensive commodity in India, something that only the well-off can afford—in marked contrast to its affordability in Europe and North America. Mothers, even the poorest of them, will do anything to give their children milk or milk products. Those who cannot are the most unfortunate of mortals. Rhyme after rhyme refers to young children, especially the favoured male child, being given bowls full of warm milk, and varied combinations of milk, rice, popped rice, bananas, mangoes, even jackfruit. In one verse, a mother calls her little boy, who answers from the kitchen garden that he is plucking greens for their midday meal. In reply, she dismisses greens as not being the right food for her beloved son, telling him instead to come inside for a meal of milk and bananas. So precious is milk, that in many verses and folktales, the cherished infant is referred to as a *kheerer putul* or a doll made of clotted cream. Another indication of the correlation between plentiful milk and familial prosperity is to be seen in recurring images of rivers or lakes of milk or cream. And with the facile transcendence of imagination, these same rivers are endowed with a wealth of fish, which the beloved son can catch and bring home.

Sometimes humour, verging on the black, is the tool for expressing the inadequacy of the provider in getting enough milk for the family's needs. In one chhara a woman describes, tongue in cheek, how the one skimpy cupful of milk she has managed to buy must be stretched to cover everyone's needs. First, it will yield two kinds of cream, as well as curds and butter, to be served at lunch and dinner. Then the two older sons will get some milk to drink, while the frothing top layer from the heated milk will be reserved for the baby. A sick relative, who suffers from a chronic cough, will get his share of the miracle fluid. Nor can the pet bird be ignored—it has such a discriminating palate that it refuses to eat birdseed. And who can forget that the head of the family must be given his share? As for the lady herself, she cannot possibly eat a meal without a bit of yoghurt!

The duality of milk and rice is also echoed in other widely lauded works of literature. In the *Annadamangalkabya*, a long narrative poem written in 1753 by Bharatchandra Ray (court poet to Maharaja Krishnachandra of Nabadwip in Bengal), a simple ferryman, who does not get swayed from the path of virtue despite the travails of poverty and want, finally receives his reward. The goddess Annada appears before him and promises to give him all he wants. True to his character, he asks, not for immense wealth, but for a guarantee that his descendants will always be able to afford rice and milk. This symbol of a desire that is modest, wholesome, and achievable is not generated entirely from the poet's fancy. It is based on a long-held regional perception about important foods.

Worshipping the numerous deities of the Hindu pantheon, those from ancient Vedic times as well as those conjured up over time by the folk imagination, is part of the daily life of rural Bengal. Although the rituals, prayers, and offerings can vary from one deity to the next, some elements are common to all such occasions of worship. They reveal a fertile artistic imagination, springing from the tropical lushness of the region. And food, as part of such rituals, acquires both literal and metaphorical relevance.

Lakshmi, the goddess of fortune, is one of the key figures worshipped in Bengal. Her importance, especially for women, is evident in the fact that not only is she worshipped with great pomp and ceremony on the night of the autumn full moon (every god or goddess is honoured on a particular day of the year), but also on every Thursday. Few Hindu homes in Bengal will be without a special niche or alcove in which an image or painting of the goddess is enshrined. And the weekly worship of Lakshmi demonstrates how blurred the line between art and prayer can be, and how food serves as both an artistic and a ceremonial medium. The rituals include the drawing of alpanas around her shrine, the symbolic offering of food for her consumption (including the essential rice as well as fruits and sweets), and the reading of a short narrative poem, the *panchali*, detailing her power and greatness. The symbolic use of rice can also be seen in the practice of filling a wicker basket with *dhan* (unhusked rice) and placing it alongside the image of the goddess. If, for some reason, the image of the goddess is absent, this basket, called *jhanpi* or *patara*, can be a substitute. And in most pictorial depictions, she appears with ears of rice in each hand.

Offerings (cooked and uncooked) made to gods and goddesses express the relevance of food in life. No puja or act of worship is complete without the making of offerings, however simple or meagre. Rice, as expected, is an integral part of such offerings. Unhusked rice and trefoil grasses (*durba*) are presented to the deities along with whole and cut fruits and other foods. The impulse of devotion is complemented with artistry. Even when a woman is worshipping the gods in the solitude of her own home, she will never set out her offerings in a slapdash fashion. Cut or peeled fruits will be arranged in circular patterns or in blocks of colour and the dhan and durba will be positioned in the middle to provide a navel-like focus. Rice pudding (*payesh*) is one of the commonest cooked items offered to the gods, combining the two universally accepted items of nourishment. Once prepared, the pudding is often decorated with *dhan* and durba before being offered. Worshipping the sun god (referred to as Itu puja or Ritu puja) is perhaps the best example of the ritual use of food grains. A late autumn event, the practice consists of filling an earthen pot with moist earth and five kinds of grains, including rice. A small copper pitcher, filled with water, is embedded in the centre of the pot. On every Sunday, for a whole month, women water the pot to allow the grains to germinate and sprout, and pray to the sun god. By the end of the month, when the harvest is in, they make rice pudding with the newly harvested rice, offer it to the god, and, finally, immerse the pot of germinating grains in a pond or river.

The same folk imagination that devised these rituals incorporating food and worship also created the secular rituals surrounding major events like weddings, births, and deaths. Food, invested with symbolism and beauty, plays a large part in some of these events. Weddings among Bengali Hindus are elaborate affairs, stretching over three days, with the preparatory rituals beginning even a week in advance. In a delta region whose rivers are prolific in fish, it is not surprising that Bengalis consider fish a symbol of plenty and use it in their wedding rituals. The Hindus of West Bengal have the custom of sending a *tattwa* or ceremonial gift presentation from the bride's family to the groom. Although the array of gifts can vary, including clothes, furniture, jewellery or sweets, the centrepiece is always a carp, decorated elaborately with oil and vermilion. The largest fish that the family can afford is acquired for this purpose and the visual totality of the apparition is stunning: gleaming, pinkish-silver scales, the dark fins and tail, the lovingly painted vermilion patterns, and the background of green (the banana leaf on which the fish rests). Milk is another symbol of plenty and some families have devised a charming custom for the bride's arrival at her in-laws'. When the groom returns with her to his family home after the wedding ceremony that took place at hers, watchful eyes coordinate her first step over the threshold with the boiling over of a pot of milk. In other families, she enters holding two small live fish in her hand, which are released in the family fishpond to breed and multiply.

As expected, the role of rice is pivotal in these rituals. Apart from the alpanas, which are joyously painted all over the house and on the piris where the bridal pair will sit, rice is also used to signify the auspiciousness of the ceremony. On the night before the wedding, women in the bride's family build a small mound of rice powder (plain or dyed), called a *sree*. This is supposed to be a symbol of Lakshmi (Sree or grace being another name for her), whose favour is essential to the success of the marriage. During the actual wedding ceremony, which entails the pair having to walk seven times around a ritual fire built by a priest, popped rice is poured by them into the fire as a prayer for prosperity. The ritual of *baran*, or welcome, is performed both when the groom arrives at the bride's house and when he returns home with her after the marriage. It is strictly a women's ritual. A large brass platter, containing flowers, leaves, the obligatory dhan and durba, and sometimes even small oil lamps, is held by the mother or other senior female relative and waved in circular motions in front of the groom or the married couple, to the accompaniment of ululation and the blowing of conch shells by other women. When major deities are worshipped on their annual festive days, priests welcome them with a similar ritual. Before they finally enter the house, the bridal pair is given something sweet to eat.

No discussion about the recurrence of food as both a theme and the raw material in indigenous Bengali art can be complete without a mention of the work of Bengali patuas or illustrators. Traditionally, every village had a resident *patua*, whose depiction of divine figures or scenes from myths, epics, and narrative poems often adorned the walls of huts, or substituted for images in the household niche reserved for worship. The illustrations were remarkable for their bold line drawings and vivid use of pure unmixed colours. The tradition of *patachitra* or *pat* (as the illustrations were called) is very old and exists throughout the Indian subcontinent. Some scholars consider the Bengali patuas to have been influenced by the miniature paintings that flourished under the Rajput and Mughal rulers in northern India. Whatever the influences, over the course of several centuries, they created a unique and unmistakable imprint that cannot be seen in any other region.

The preparation of paper and colour for painting shows again how integrated rice was with the expression of the artistic impulse of Bengal. Glue, prepared by boiling crushed rice, was first applied to individual sheets of paper. Ten or twelve such sheets were successively glued together to form a thick pad, which was further hardened by being pressed over a wooden board by a stone pestle applied like a rolling pin. Once the pad was dry and stiff, the patua could start the painting. The bold, vibrant colours used in illustrations were derived from natural substances like indigo, cinnabar, chalk, vermilion, soot from an oil lamp and burnt rice, crushed and made into a paste with water. Each of these was carefully mixed in a solution made from the gum of tamarind or a fruit called *bel*.

The subjects favoured by most rural illustrators were, as demanded by their clients, mostly sacred—scenes from the Ramayana and the Mahabharata, episodes from the life of Krishna or from the life of Sri Chaitanya. But one branch of this art shows considerable urban influence and was highly secular in content, rich in acute social commentary. This is the body of indigenous paintings known as the Kalighat pats, produced by illustrators who settled around the Kali temple in Kalighat, Calcutta. Although the temple was built in 1809, the site had been dedicated to the Goddess Kali since the fifteenth century. Rural patuas, looking for more work, started settling there from the middle of the eighteenth century. Most were from the district of Medinipur in Bengal. As the city of Calcutta grew under the British and its Bengali residents developed the distinct 'babu' culture, the illustrators gave full play to their artistic imagination by depicting different aspects of urban life. Eventually, their work spawned the famous woodcut prints that vividly illustrated the genre of cheap romantic thrillers published by the local Battala press.

One of the best collections of Kalighat pats can be found in the Victoria and Albert Museum in London. During colonial rule, the paintings travelled across the oceans as part of the collections of British civil servants and missionaries. The collection in the Victoria and Albert Museum contains several pats which belonged to J. Lockwood Kipling, father of Rudyard and for many years Principal of the Lahore School of Arts (now in Pakistan).

The Kalighat paintings project the image of a society in flux, where the men, who were in the external world, were caught between the servility demanded by their colonial masters and the libertine pursuit of sensory pleasures. Amoral attitudes and double standards were highly prevalent. On the other hand, women, imprisoned in the home, continued the rural, ritualistic traditions of their forebears. Many of these rituals involved the elaborate preparation of food and the Kalighat artists frequently focused on that. Ceremonies like *jamaishashthi* (honouring the son-in-law) or *bhaiphonta* (sisters praying for the welfare of their brothers and feeding them a special meal) are common subjects of pats. Inevitably, they centre on food—a large plate of rice and condiments surrounded by numerous bowls containing an array of fish, meat, legumes, vegetables, chutneys, and desserts. But beyond the literal depiction lies the significance of the effort behind these elaborate, multi-course meals (the ideal feast was supposed to consist of sixty-four dishes). For the son-in-law, the effort was in the nature of a tribute—an offering made to the person who held the happiness, comfort, even the life of a beloved daughter in his hands. In the case of the brother, it was an act of appeasement—the sister praying to avert the attentions of the god of death. In a male-dominated society, a brother's death was an evil to be feared; no one cared about the sister's well-being.

Even more remarkable are the pats with vivid, intimate close-ups conveying specific messages. A man's hand clasps huge blue-black freshwater prawns, a medium-sized carp, and a *lau* or bottle gourd. The combination of gourd and prawns, which will produce the classic *lau-chingri*, is a commentary on the Bengali preoccupation with food—a fact well-noted in other parts of India. Another drawing, titled 'Biral Tapaswi' (the ascetic cat), shows up the hypocrisy of many urban Bengalis who hid their dissolute habits under a surface sobriety. The image is that of a cat whose forehead and nose bear the markings typical of holy ascetics who espouse a strictly vegetarian diet. But in its mouth, the cat holds a large prawn, which, obviously, it plans to devour in secrecy.

Aside from the works of illustrators, all the artistic endeavours surrounding the life and rituals of Bengal stand out in their carefree assumption of impermanence. Objects and spaces are decorated with great intensity of effort and imagination, although the artist knows that the work will vanish within days. Verses she composes will never be attributed to her and will possibly undergo subtle mutations in oral transmission. Accepting this transience as the inevitable fate of art resonates well with the choice of food items as either the raw material for art or the means of expressing—through metaphor and symbolism—the ritual significance of life. As long as the land endured, these foods would keep on being generated. That assurance was enough to stimulate the robust and prolific imagination of Bengal. Anchored in a fertile alluvial delta, nourished by the richness of its natural resources, spanning the belief systems of animism and deism, Bengal's artistry has taken the sustenance of daily living and shaped it into a medium for investing life with meaning and ceremony.

REFERENCES

ACHAYA, K.T. *Indian Food, A Historical Companion*. Delhi: Oxford University Press, 1998.

BAHADUR, Om Lata. *The Book of Hindu Festivals and Ceremonies*. New Delhi: UBS Publishers-Distributors Ltd., 1994.

BANERJEE, Amiya Kumar. *West Bengal District Gazetteers: Hooghly*. Calcutta: Government of West Bengal, 1972.

BEINOS, S. C. *Twenty-four Plates Illustrative of Hindoo and European Manners in Bengal*. Calcutta: Riddhi, 1832

BIRMINGHAM, David. *A Concise History of Portugal*. Cambridge: Cambridge University Press, 1993.

CAMPBELL-PLATT, Geoffrey. *Fermented Foods of the World: A Dictionary and Guide*. London: Butterworths, 1987.

CARR, SANDY. *The Simon and Schuster Pocket Guide to Cheese*. New York: Simon and Schuster, 1981.

CHAKRABARTI, Mukundaram. *Chandimangalkavya*. Calcutta: Bharabi, 1992.

DAS Anathnath and Bishwanath Ray, eds. *Chhelebhulano Chhara*. Calcutta: Ananda Publishers, 1995.

DAS, Jnanendramohan. *Bangla Bhashar Abhidhaan*. [Allahabad: Indian Press, 1937]; Calcutta: Sahitya Samsad, 1986.

DUTT, Gurusaday. *Folk Arts and Crafts of Bengal: The Collected Papers*, Calcutta: Seagull Books, 1990.

GUPTA, R. P. 'Purano Kolkatar Katkhodai Chhabi.' *Amrita*

(Autumn Special), 1981.

KABIRAJ, Krishnadas. *Chaitanyacharitamrita* (Atulkrishna Goswami, ed.). Calcutta: Bangabasi Press (4th edition), 1927.

MATHERS, Powys, tr. (from original French version by Dr. J. C. Madrus). *The Book of Thousand Nights and One Night*. London: Routledge, 1996.

MITRA, Sudhir Kumar. *Hooghly Jelar Itihash o Bangasamaj*, vol. 2. Calcutta: Mitrani Prakashan, 1963.

MITRA-MAJUMDAR, Dakshhinaranjan. *Thakurmar Jhuli*. Calcutta: Mitra & Ghosh Publishers Pvt. Ltd., 1996.

MUKHOPADHYAY, Bipradas. *Mishtanno Pak*. Calcutta: Ananda Publishers (reprint of original 1906 edition), 1981.

O'FLAHERTY, Wendy Doniger, tr. (from the original Sanskrit). *Hindu Myths*. London: Penguin Books, 1975.

ORTIZ, Elisabeth Lambert. *The Food of Spain and Portugal*. New York: Atheneum, 1989.

PAUL, Ashit, ed. *Woodcut Prints of Nineteenth Century Calcutta*. Calcutta: Seagull Books, 1983.

RAY, Bharatchandra. *Annadamangalkabya* (Kartik Bhadra, ed.). Calcutta: S. Banerjee and Co., 1985.

RAY, Niharranjan. *Bangalir Itihaas*. Calcutta: Dey's Publishing, 1993.

TAGORE, Abanindranath. *Kheerer Putul*. Calcutta: Ananda Publishers (12th edition), 1997.

ACKNOWLEDGEMENTS

Portions of this book have previously appeared in print—though in considerably different versions. The introduction and chapters 3 and 7 are based on columns written for the *Boston Globe*, Food Section. Portions of chapters 4 and 5 were published in an essay in *Petits Propos Culinaires*, Prospect Books Ltd., London. A different version of chapter 6 was published as an article in *Gastronomica*—the journal of food and culture published by University of California Press, Berkeley. Chapter 8 was published in *Granta 52*, a special issue on food. Chapters 9 and 10 were papers presented at the Oxford Symposium on Food and Cookery in 1999 and 1998, respectively.

I would like to thank Louise Kennedy, former editor of the *Boston Globe* Food Section for her support and encouragement and Anjum Katyal at Seagull Books for her creative vision.

Chitrita Banerji

All photographs in this book are by Naveen Kishore. The photographs are of: the Jhamapukur Rajbati, Raja Digambar Mitra's house, at 1 Jhamapukur Lane (courtesy Supriyo Ghosh); Manmatha Nath Mitra's house, at 34 Shyampukur Street, now the residence of Smt Smriti Mitter (courtesy Smriti Mitter); and Khelat Ghosh's house, at 47 Pathuriaghata Street, now the residence of Mr Pradip Ghose (courtesy Pradip Ghose). The publishers gratefully acknowledge the helpful cooperation of Ms Sukanya Ghosh in making these spaces accessible.